D0984268

March '07
Dear Peggy
Hope this awakens
happy memories
Eleanor

Tales of Bequia

Thomas Carl Thomsen

Cross River Press • P.O. Box 473, Cross River, NY 10518 • 914-763-8030

TALES OF BEQUIA. Copyright © 1988 by
Thomas Carl Thomsen. All rights reserved.
Printed in the United States of America. No part of
this book may be used or reproduced in any manner
whatsoever without written permission except in
the case of brief quotations embodied in critical
reviews or articles. For information address Cross
River Press, PO Box 473, Cross River, NY 10518

Design by Armando Carloni.

Sketches by Frank Crosio.

Library of Congress Cataloging in Publications Data.

Thomsen, Thomas Carl.

Tales of Bequia/Thomas Carl Thomsen. -- 1st ed.
p.   cm.
Includes index.

ISBN 0-945288-00-X: $12.95

1. Bequia Island (St. Vincent and the Grenadines) --
Description and travel. 2. Bequia Island
(St. Vincent and the Grenadines) -- Social life and
customs. I. Thomsen, Thomas Carl. II. Title.
972.98'44--dc19

Dedicated to kindred spirits
in search of paradise.

CONTENTS

BEQUIA

This book is about Bequia, an unusual island in the Caribbean, and about people who have come to the island in search of something. A new life. Fulfillment. Escape. Paradise. It is also about some Bequians with similar aspirations. Transplants or natives, they have this in common: their lives have taken on a new meaning. I think the island is magical. Those who have not been caught in its web may disagree.

The first time I approached Bequia from the open sea I was reminded of the passage from Childe Harold's Pilgrimage, "Are not the mountains, waves, and skies a part of me as I of them?" The hills ahead of me were as green as a St. Vincent parrot. The seas were deep blue and in closer to shore they became light green and I could see the coral and multicolored fish below so clearly that I seemed to be gliding through nothingness. The sky? Look at an artist's pallet for the brightest blue. Then for the fleecy cirrus clouds that hardly

1

move across the sky, dab swirls of almost transparent white. The hills and the sea and the sky fitted together quite perfectly and I got the feeling of oneness and that I belonged.

Bequia could be the figment of one's imagination, but it is not. It really exists, despite the denials of travel agents who prefer to deal with more tangible things like package tours.

Geographers will tell you that Bequia is near the end of the archipelago that begins with Cuba, fans eastward and southward in a large crescent for more than 1500 miles and ends in Trinidad. Sometimes called the gem of the Grenadines, it is about nine miles south of St. Vincent, the mother island of the Grenadines, and one hundred miles west of Barbados.

When you walk the island, you become quickly aware that it is hilly and irregularly shaped, consisting of coral and volcanic outcroppings, rugged peaks, steep ravines, and deeply embayed harbors. It is only nine miles long, but it would take days to walk it.

The outside world is hundreds of light years removed from Bequia. The travails of the world do not matter much here. Concerns are very basic: fishing for grouper, kingfish, and an occasional whale; raising chickens, cows, sheep and goats; planting and cultivating kitchen gardens to provide some of the basic necessities; catching rainwater on the roof and storing it in cisterns; harvesting coconuts and bananas on the few remaining plantations; dressing the children properly for school and church; telling stories under the almond tree in the harbor; and enjoying an occasional strong rum in one of the many small shops that dispense both groceries

2

and beverages.

The island's quiet, easy, almost carefree life-style has great appeal, at least for those who would like progress to stand still for a moment, so that they can take stock of their lives. It is easy to manage change here, since it takes place at a turtle-pace.

The sugar mill at Spring still stands, although in ruins, covered now by bougainvillea and hibiscus. The plantation continues to be worked, but the canefields have been plowed under. In the distance you can see a square rigged schooner sailing in out of the past, and you can dig in the sand at the beach for remnants of the Arawak civilization that existed long before Columbus discovered the islands. As I stand on the beach at Spring, I sense that little has changed. I am alone on the crescent-shaped beach, bordered by towering coconut trees, sea grapes and manshaniel. Birds race along the beach, as the sea recedes, looking for sea life washed ashore, just as they have done for hundreds of years, maybe thousands.

Meeting the Punnet family is like stepping into the past. Langley and Margaret live in an old plantation house on the northeast end of the island which is the lushest and least inhabited part of the island. They have gotten back to basics, like growing vegetables and fruit, raising chickens, producing eggs for the several inns on the island. Recently, they started to raise pigs which they say are very clean and smart. Electricity hasn't reached them, so their home is lighted by candles and kerosene lamps. Like their colonizing ancestors (the Punnet family came to St. Vincent in 1713), they live by the sun, rising early and retiring early. Their move to Bequia occurred about ten years ago when investments on St. Vincent went bad.

Langley's experience with pigs is very recent and he approaches it with the enthusiasm of a person much younger than his 60 odd years of age. I was fascinated when he told me that his pigs, free to wander, would regularly go down to the beach, roll in the sand, and then splash about in the sea.

"You know, Tom," he said in his part-Vincentian, part-English accent, "I have a big black sow who regularly disappears and returns in foal days later. Last time I followed her all the way to Spring, about a mile and a half away. She has a boy friend there, who obliges. Finally, she comes home." He paused. "A liberated sow, wouldn't you say?"

Langley doesn't show the scars from having lost one of the finest plantations on St. Vincent, a hotel, and a golf club. His typically English reserve disguises whatever bitterness he may feel. By Vincentian standards he is an aristocrat, with fine breeding, impeccable manners, keen intelligence, and the self-assurance derived from a proper bringing up and education abroad.

"Have you ever been beyond my home to Sharks Bay and the Bullet?" he said.

I confessed that I hadn't. "I understand it can be dangerous."

"Not really, if you know what you are doing. There's an unfinished road out there that leads part of the way through the jungle to an old sugar mill and the foundations of a house. The road was built by the French hundreds of years ago. It was very well built and is quite usable. I would like to finish the road someday."

Margaret, his wife, was also born on St. Vincent. Her

4

mother, Daphne, was born in England, and she married Major Peter Harley, who spent forty years in the Colonial service before retiring. They live most of the year in East Sussex, England, and have a vacation home on Mount Pleasant in Bequia. His last post before retiring was Chief of Police of St. Vincent, when it was a colony. You could almost guess that he had held a post of this sort from his appearance. He has an inscrutable look. He looks at you through partly closed, somewhat slanted eyes, that seem to be constantly searching.

Margaret is the product of Daphne's earlier marriage to a Vincentian. That probably explains her complexion which is more French than English. She is striking looking. Tall, black hair, brown eyes that twinkle, and a strong handsome face. She is not afraid to put her hands in the soil and she is as determined as her husband to make a success of what may be their last best chance.

I admire people who are not afraid or reluctant to work manually. The work ethic has become a little obsolete back home, but not here. Julie McIntosh, who runs Julie's Guest House together with his wife, Isola, has a sign over his bar which states, "Stamp out poverty. Work."

Langley talked about the unfinished road on several subsequent occasions. I got the impression that the road was some sort of symbol. A target. An objective. An ideal. Perhaps like Moby Dick. Or Virginia Wolff's Lighthouse. When you are away from the travails of everyday life, you can conjure with such possibilities as these. Bequia is the right place to let your thoughts run free.

The whole north end of the island was once owned by

four McIntosh brothers, who had been bequeathed the land by their father. Only one still owns his inheritance and that is Bunty, who lives in Trinidad. His estate is called Raintree, a peninsula covered with cedars and raintrees that have been sculpted into patterns by the relentless trade winds. Sidney McIntosh sold Park and Industry estates to an American, named Wagner, and to Langley. One of the brothers sold his estate a number of years ago for a car. There is little land as beautiful and majestic as this left in the world and one day soon it will be worth millions.

Sidney is now dead. He passed on a few years after his wife, Enid, who was as retiring as Sidney was outgoing. Sidney was a big Scotsman with red hair and a red beard. He fancied himself a Don Juan and probably was. I remember several years after Enid's death Sidney had a hundred copies made of his favorite photo of himself standing in majestic profile in the garden of his typically English home. Across the bottom of the photograph he wrote ''Alone.'' He sent a copy to most of the women friends he had ever met. Apparently, he received a fair response, for he was kept quite busy entertaining.

I recall the marvelous parties that Sidney and Enid gave almost weekly during the tourist season. The parties were on the front terrace where the fragrances of the English garden and the sounds of the surf and the constant trade winds rustling through the coconut fronds thrilled the senses.

When the attention he received from his mailing of ''Alone'' began to decline, so did Sidney. He was in his late seventies when he died. It happened quickly. And unexpectedly because no one ever considered that this rambunctious

6

party-thrower and party-goer would ever depart from the Bequia scene.

One memory is quite amusing. A dinner dance was held at the Windward Islands Greathouse to help raise funds to build a school. It was an all-out affair and it went on until daybreak. The following afternoon I found Sidney in an early stage of recovery sprawled in his planter's chair.

"Gawd, what a party!" he exclaimed. "I lost my Landrover and my teeth. Well, I found my car next to Barclays and there under the car was a dog chewing on my teeth! I shouted the beast away and retrieved my teeth, which fortunately were still in good shape. See?" He gave a broad grin.

I have many memories of Enid and Sidney, who were lovely friends and neighbors. I remember when Enid was dying she had her bed moved to one of the front rooms so that she could see the blossoms of the frangipani in the front yard and the bougainvillea climbing around the window and almost into her room and watch the hummingbirds and banana twits hovering around the bougainvillea and hear the rumbling sea. She knew she was dying, and she died gracefully, like everything else she did.

Her burial at the graveyard in the harbor lasted the better part of the day. After the service at the Anglican Church, her casket was brought to the cemetery a few hundred yards away. The service was brief and then the singing began. It went on all morning and afternoon. There were rival choral groups. When one stopped, another would start up, and so it went on late into the day. I remember Sidney wandering around, seemingly at a loss, perspiring profusely from the very hot tropic sun. Finally, it ended, when the choral groups seemingly called it a draw, and exhausted, departed.

Their lovely home close to the beach at Industry is still unoccupied. Their children in the States and their spouses haven't much interest in a place so remote and primitive as Bequia. What a pity. I guess that when something extraordinary comes easily, it isn't extraordinary.

The road from the McIntosh home at Industry rises gradually from sea level to a height of about a hundred feet, bends around Crown Point, and then drops off to beach level at Spring. From Crown Point, you get a good view of the peninsula called Raintree. There's a dirt road that runs from the plantation area to the end of the peninsula. Part of the road has dropped into the sea, as a result of the relentless pounding of the surf. The flat area of the estate, which borders the road to the harbor, is very fertile. It is used primarily to grow coconut and to pasture cows, goats, and sheep. George Gooding used to be overseer of the plantation. I would see him almost every time I walked through the plantation and along the shore to the harbor. He was small and frail but he was a survivor. At age eighty he was still overseer. I remember him in his blue dungarees and Wellington boots, always carrying a cutlass. His face was weatherbeaten and he spoke softly in an accent that only the older whites had. He was a proud man. Proud of his island, his family, his work. He said to me one day, "Tom, you know I have a big family. Guess how big." I told him I couldn't. "Last count there were close to eighty children, grand children, and great grandchildren." He had good reason to be proud. All the Goodings I know are hard working and responsible.

George is in his nineties now. He doesn't work at the plantation any more, but he still takes walks, which are getting shorter each year. I still meet up with him. I remember that the last time we met, I was so glad to see him I grabbed him by his shoulders. His body was frail and boney and I felt a little embarrassed. I sensed his days might be numbered and I did not like that.

The road to the harbor, as it passes through Spring Plantation, is lined with yellow and orange pride of barbados and white oleander, and there next to the ruins of the old sugar mill, several large frangipani trees fully in bloom with large orange blossoms. There are many frangipanies on the island, white as well as orange. It is believed that the tree was brought to the island from the South Seas, much the way the breadfruit tree was transplanted by the legendary Captain Blighe. The original breadfruit tree, incidentally, still grows in the tropical gardens on St. Vincent.

As you walk along the road, through Raintree Estate, there is a large stand of coconut trees on the left and an open pasture on the right. You see here some fine specimens of Holstein and Jersey cattle, plus sheep and goats. Many of the animals live in the pasture, others are brought by local people from the harbor to graze and are led back to the harbor at the end of the day. The sounds you hear are the waves breaking along the closeby shore, the birds chirping, and the tethered cows bellowing and sheep bleating. When you meet someone on this road, she is carrying something on her head, perhaps a sack of home-made charcoal, or he is carrying a cutlass, the all purpose implement used for cutting and digging. I like walking on this road, because I know most of the people I pass. By their greetings, I know that I am welcome on their island.

When you reach the saddle in the hill, with Cinnamon Gardens on your right and the road to Hope on your left, the landscape changes abruptly. The idyllic countryside is behind you and now you face the bustling harbor ahead and below. The hillside is dotted with homes painted in bright hues of blue, yellow, and green, and every home seems to have an abundance of noisy chickens and wherever there is a spare blade of grass you find a tethered goat grazing. Most every homeowner has a kitchen-garden and many tropical plants that need no attention, grow wild and bloom forever. In the early morning, as day breaks, you hear first an isolated rooster as you walk down the road from the saddle between the hills to the harbor, and then another, and then more and finally the harbor is alive with their crowing. Households are awakened and lights go on and dogs begin to bark and you hear the sounds of families moving about in their modest homes.

The harbor is considered one of the best in the world. It forms a large "U", providing almost complete protection, and it is deep enough to permit large boats to come very close to shore. You are likely to find boats from all over the world anchored in the harbor. The most exotic in my experience was a Dhow that had been sailed from Turkey. Sail boats of all sizes easily make the trip from Europe in 30 days or so. It is not a novelty anymore to meet a young couple, with a child, who have traveled in a 25 foot sailboat from England. Hillery and Neal Sanders were such a couple. He became principal of the new high school and she taught navigation.

Navigation would be a unique subject in a school in the States. But Bequia is a seafarer's island. It is the last of the Caribbean islands to hunt whales. Many of its inhabitants are fishermen, and also as many go to sea on merchant ships. Next to the altar in the beautiful Anglican Church is a painting of Christ. In one hand Christ is holding a sailboat. A small black boy standing at his side reaches across Christ to touch the boat.

The Bequian's love affair with the sea began around the middle 1800s. Slavery was ended by an Act of Parliament in 1838. Sugar production went into a slump as a result and never regained its position as a major crop. Whaling came into the picture at this time and helped to offset the decline in sugar production and employment.

Fishing, whaling, boat-building, going to sea on contract are so deeply entrenched in their psyche that there really are no alternatives. A land-based job like working on roads or on a plantation? Most Bequians would prefer to sit idly under the almond tree in the harbor, waiting for a seafaring job to come along, rather than work on the land.

Main street follows the shore line. There are a number of colorful shops here, including two grocery stores, Sams and S & W, which, while small, are patterned after our self-service markets and have one advantage in that they deal in intoxicating beverages as well as groceries; Wallaces dry goods store; several boutiques; a ships chandlery; a number of rum bars with such names as the New York Bar and the New Jersey Bar; and Julie's Guest House which serves some of the best food on the island. While Julie's name hangs over the entrance, it is really run by his very capable wife, Isola.

Julie's main interest is building homes, at which he is very good.

Next to Julie's Guest House is the District Council Building, where you pay taxes and complain about trash collection, which is getting better. There still are times when either the truck or the driver is sick, or the driver has run out of gas, but they are fewer in number. Across from Julie's is the fish market, a small rectangular building with screening on three sides from chest-height to the ceiling. When you hear the blowing of a conch shell that is the signal that fish have been brought ashore and are for sale. Next to the fish market is an open vegetable and fruit market, consisting of a small shack and a number of crates of fruits and vegetables on the ground or on stands made of boxes placed on end. The market is run by a group of rastafarians from St. Vincent, who perform a needed service but are not particularly well liked by other merchants. Rastas, as they are called, are said to be members of a religious sect that was started by Emperor Haillie Selasie in Ethiopia. Rastas are easily identified by their dreadlocks, which look menacing and are usually concealed by a large wool cap. The Rastas seldom mingle with the Bequians and are content to exist independently, running what appears to be a very profitable business. Closeby is the tourist center, a one room building, at the foot of the main dock, where you catch the Friendship Rose or any of the other boats providing passage to St. Vincent.

The area beyond the dock for a distance of about 150 yards is used by taxi drivers in the tourist season. A favored place for the drivers to gather while waiting for a fare is under a very large almond tree, which provides ample protection against the sun's rays. A stone bench has been built around the base of the tree for the comfort of visitors, provided they get there before the drivers. The area has been nicely planted and kept by the government. There is a beach here that extends all the way to the Frangipani. It is one of the beaches where you are likely to see examples of Bequia boat-building. Occasionally you will see a large vessel careened off shore. The method of careening hasn't changed in hundreds of years. A vessel is brought close to shore at high tide. When the tide lowers, the boat is rolled over on its side and the bottom is scraped clean. It is righted on the next high tide and rolled over on its clean side for the other side to be scraped. On the next high tide it is righted and pushed out to deeper waters.

Across the street from the Anglican Church is the inevitable Barclays Bank and farther along Mrs. Taylor's grocery store, the Bosuns Shop, the Workshop of the Handicapped, and the Schools for the Deaf and the Handicapped. From here you walk along the water's edge to reach the Frangipani, an inn owned by the Prime Minister of St. Vincent and the Grenadines, James "Son" Mitchell, and run by his wife, Pat.

Both Son and Pat are very much involved with the island. One of her current projects is to build a whaling museum. Son has two big commitments as Prime Minister: one, to rebuild the roads, which are badly in need of repair; and the second, to build a small airport. Talk of an airport has gone on for many years, so many locals are betting it will never happen. They argue that it is too big a project for such a small island. Also, nothing big has ever succeeded on Bequia. They cite the Bequia Inn as an example. It was to be a big, modern hotel on Friendship Bay. It was near completion when the developers from Canada ran out of money and abandoned the project. Bequians did benefit but in their fashion. Doors, windows, pots, pans, chairs, beds, things that were not nailed down simply walked away, as the expression goes. There seems to be some kind of supernatural force at work designed to keep the island from moving too far too fast. Most everyone on the island likes it this way.

Supporters of the airport argue that it would help greatly in emergencies. To get to a hospital now, one has to charter a speedboat and suffer a bumpy and wet ride to St. Vincent, about nine miles away. Son wants the airport because it will benefit Bequians and attract tourists. A politician of uncommon ability, he is fine-tuned to the realities of the world about him. An airport on Bequia could only add to his image as a leader who gets results.

At home, milling about the Frangipani Inn, he looks like anyone but a politician. His dress is usually very informal and he is accessible to almost anyone. Family has been very important to him. For years he spent a lot of time with his children as they were growing up. Now they are in Canada on the verge of becoming young adults.

Let me give you a little more background about this unusual island. According to the last census, which is several years old, there are 4400 people on Bequia, and most are descendants of the slaves who were brought to Bequia in the 1600s and 1700s to grow sugar and cotton, and the Carib Indians who fought for control and finally gave in to the English in 1795. As a result of intermarriage with Scotch, English and French settlers, complexions range from very white to very black. Many of the whites are descendants of the Scots who came in the late 1700s and early 1800s and live mostly on Mount Pleasant, the highest hill on Bequia. In Paget Farm, the features of the Carib Indian, with his deep set eyes and high cheekbones, are blended with a mixture of French and black blood lines.

Cultural differences among Bequians have become blurred. Families have tended to become clans. The Ollivierres live at Paget and La Pomp, the Davises on Mount Pleasant, the Simmonds at Lower Bay, and the Wallaces and Mitchells in Port Elizabeth and Friendship, each with its own distinct family tree, facial characteristics, and special positions on the island.

The mores of the island concerning marriage allow considerable latitude and generally favor the male. A man and woman may live together for many years without getting married. If they decide to marry, it may not be until after the third child. It is not unusual for the male to have more than one family: an inside family, if he is married, and one or more outside families. There is an important benefit to marriage from the male point of view if his wife has property: her property becomes his. It is unlikely that the marriage mores are likely to change anytime soon. No one seems to object to them, and so far there are no libbers on the island to agitate for change.

You can find remnants of the African culture that was brought over by slaves many years ago. Many of the people have memories of ring parties, where people would form a circle around a fire, dance to drums, and tell stories. The memories are kept alive by songs, as for example this passage from Evening Time:

Evening time, work is over now, its evening time.
We da go 'pon mountain, da go 'pon mountain,
Da go 'pon mountainside.
Now we done an' we glad work time done,
We go eat an' drink, dance, an' play ring thing
On the mountainside.

Jumbies still exist for most Bequians. Jumbies are spirits. They usually take the male form and are dressed in black and wear a high hat. They can be benevolent or malevolent, mostly the latter. They live in the woods, under bridges, and sometimes in the trunks of trees. They are to be avoided at all costs.

Bequians are quick to tell you that Bequians do not steal. They say that if you're missing something, somebody from some other island is responsible. For the uninitiated, it may be difficult to tell the difference between stealing and borrowing. If you are missing something and you find it in someone else's possession, he is likely to explain that you weren't using it and he needed it. I remember returning to the island one time and finding two tires of my Moke missing. It wasn't difficult to find out who had them. Most everyone knew. And when I confronted that person, he simply explained that I wasn't using them and he needed them. He happily, without any embarrassment whatever, returned the tires and went on his business.

Bequians tend to be easy-going people. But they can be aroused by events big and small. When it comes to politics, there is no middle ground. You are either for the party or against it and feelings can run very high. When a campaign is on, friends can become enemies and afterwards the wounds

16

take a long time to heal. Politics seem to occupy a position in their consciousness at the same level as family and church.

When aroused, their response is sometimes exaggerated. I remember one time I was having dinner with my family at Spring Hotel. All of a sudden a procession burst on the scene. A line of agitated, excited, noisy Bequians passed along the walk just outside the dining area. They carried sticks and brooms, and they were led by Julie, who carried a shot gun. They were headed, I learned, for one of the bedrooms close to the dining room to deal with a Conga snake that had gotten into the room and was ensconced on an exposed rafter. My son joined the procession, and fortunately, because when he reached the room he found that Julie was prepared to blow it off the rafters with his shotgun. He persuaded Julie to let him try to get the four foot snake with his spear gun. He fetched the gun quickly. Silence descended as he took aim. He shot the snake right through the head and it fell dead on the floor. The quiet was over. The room rocked with shouts of approval, vented anger and vengeance. The snake was quite dead but everyone who crowded into the room seized the opportunity to beat it with a broom or a stick or anything handy. They partied a bit afterwards and then dispersed into the quiet of the night.

An incident occurred during my first visit to the island which is still vivid in my mind. My wife, granddaughter and I thought we'd take in a movie. The movie house was unlike anything I had every seen. It was in a big, old building that had probably been a warehouse at one time. When we approached the entrance, a confrontation was taking place between a very big man and a half dozen of his followers and an even bigger man who was taking tickets. The problem arose because the big man with his followers wanted to go in and had no tickets and the bigger man at the door refused them admittance. They were nose to nose and excited.

"Ise goin in!" the intruder shouted.

"No, ya aint!" was the response.

"Ah is!"

"Ya aint!"

It went on like this a few more times. Then abrupt silence. Finally, as quickly as it began, it ended. The big man and his followers disappeared. Occasionally you run into confrontations like this and they all seem to end the same way, no violence, just an angry glare and then silence.

The movie house was packed with noisy, happy people. A waitress at Spring Hotel had made some kind of arrangement for us to sit up front. How she was able to hold three seats, I have no idea. It was going to be difficult for our grandchild to get through the mass of bodies, so without any notice, she was picked up and passed overhead to the front of the theatre and placed in her seat. When we finally got to our seats, she was quite composed and amused.

Seeing a movie on Bequia is a unique experience. Most everyone in the audience becomes involved in the action on the screen. They are in and out of their seats shouting instructions, approval, disapproval, warnings, and encouragement to the people on the screen. When it was over I realized that the audience had been through a cathartic experience, not unlike what the Greek tragedians had in mind in staging a play.

When you consider the history of the island, it is

surprising that Bequians are as easy-going as they are. If records existed, some could probably trace their origins to the slaves on board the Palmira, a slave ship, which was grounded off the shores of Bequia in 1675. The ship sank and its cargo of blacks reached shore and were welcomed by the Carib Indians. In time the blacks and Indians intermarried and produced a tribe of black Caribs who proved even more rebellious than the yellow Caribs and succeeded in instigating constant conflict between the French and the English. The island of St. Vincent, including Bequia, changed ownership six times in the three hundred years between their discovery by Columbus and 1795 when the conflicts finally ended. The Caribs never agreed to the changes in control and fiercely defended their rights as the original settlers. They massacred the French in 1654, conspired with the French when the English were in control and with the English when the French ran things, and were responsible for the islands being declared a neutral state in 1748 when the English and French realized they could reach no accommodation with the Caribs.

A central figure in the contests in the late 1700s between the English and French was a black Carib who spoke French and had a French name, Chatoyer. Inspired by a French radical, Victor Hughes, who brought word of the success of the French revolution in overturning tyranny, Chatoyer joined forces with the French and attacked the English. His followers considered him invincible. He was intelligent, charismatic, and probably was influenced by his own legend of invincibility. He challenged British Major Leith to a duel and was killed.

Following his death, a last ditch effort was made in 1795 to oust the English, but it failed. The Caribs were trapped by the English and 5085 were captured and shipped first to Bequia and then to Honduras. From that time on Caribs ceased to be a force in the Grenadines and the English remained firmly in control.

A well known name in the Caribbean and Bequia is Warner. The family owned large tracts of land on Bequia in the 1700s and 1800s and raised sugar and cotton. The family name goes back much farther. An ancestor, Thomas Warner, came to Guiana in the early 1600s to raise tobacco, but he lost his patent, left Guiana to sail north to the Lesser Antilles. He tried to grow tobacco on St. Vincent but was unsuccessful because of excessive rain and he travelled farther north and reached St. Kitts in 1624 where he settled and raised tobacco and a family that spread its wings over much of the Caribbean.

It was a Warner, Sarahann Warner, from St. Vincent, who married Lieutenant William Thomas Wallace, an English naval officer sent to St. Vincent to reestablish the laws of the sea which apparently were being flouted by American pirates following the War of 1812. They moved to Bequia, had a son, William Thomas Wallace II, in 1840, who went to England to study navigation and got a job with the Hughes Trading Company. He returned to Bequia, where he and his brother inherited the Friendship Estate. He joined a whaler and left ship when it returned to New England. There he met an American girl, Stella Curran, daughter of a Yankee whaling captain. He returned to Friendship with his wife shortly before 1870, the year his first son was born, and in 1875 he began whaling for the hump back whales.

The Frangipani is the center of activity on the island. There is a constant stream of people passing along the terrace of the Frangipani, going from the harbor to points farther south and then later returning. There is a kidney-shaped table next to the bar, which is a favorite place to rest and have a refreshment. If you sit there long enough, you'll meet most everyone on the island. Since we don't have a newspaper, it serves quite adequately as a center for the exchange of information. Violet Wallach, who has been coming to Bequia for the past thirty years, is editor ex officio. If she doesn't know what is going on, it isn't worth knowing.

Beyond the Frangipani is a string of colorful, West Indian shops and restaurants that are reached by a path along the edge of the beach. Next to the Frangipani is the Whalebone Bar and Restaurant, with its whalebone bar and stools; then the Green Boley, which sells the best rottis on the island (rottis are curried beef or conch in a folded crepe); Mac's Pizza, featuring lobster, conch, and other exotic pizzas; Goff's Fig Tree, a restaurant and guest house; the Crabhole, which sells casual clothes, gifts, and silk screened fabrics made on the premises; and finally the Sunny Caribee, a beautiful West Indian Inn, with many cottages that blend into the hibiscus and bougainvillea. The buildings along the route are all different, some made of bamboo, others of stone and weathered shingle, but they all fit together exotically.

Farther along, beyond the Sunny Caribee and around the point at Belmont, is one of the loveliest beaches on Bequia, Princess Margaret Beach, so named because Princess

Margaret once stepped foot on it. It was previously called Tony Gibbons beach. Many prefer to call it by its original name since the Princess is not very popular on Bequia. Besides, she prefers Mustique, the next island where she has a home. The next beach is called Lower Bay and it stretches for better than a mile bordered by seagrapes, cedar, coconut trees, and occasionally a manshaniel. There is a little private school at the end of the beach appropriately named the Lower Bay School, which has an enrollment of about sixty children from families of better than average means. The School for the Handicapped and the School for the Deaf used to be located here but were moved to the harbor a few years ago. The Bequia Mission, a Canadian group headed by Father Ron Ron Armstrong and his wife, June, is the sponsor of the two schools.

The climate becomes drier as you travel into the southern and western areas. The sea at Friendship Bay, which faces south east, is rougher than on the Caribbean side of the island, and yet it has one of the best beaches on the island, stretching for more than a mile in a large crescent. At one end, on the side of a hill, the Mitchell sons recently built an island schooner. At the opposite end of the crescent are two whale-boats, a collection of fishing boats, and seine nets drying in the sun.

On the side of a hill, just above the beach, is Jimmy's and Sandy's house. Jimmy is Jimmy Carville who designed and built the house, and Sandy is Sandy Meisner, who helped to found the Group Theatre in the 30s and later established himself as one of the country's leading drama teachers. They share the house and spend most of the year there, returning to New York occasionally where Sandy still teaches at the Neighborhood Playhouse. Still teaches, because he lost his voice box to cancer a few years back. Most anyone else would have given up under the circumstances.

Farther along the road is La Pomp, where the whalers live. Athneal Ollivierre is the last of the harpooners. He lives in a gray, weather-beaten house, alongside the road, not far from the whaleboats on Friendship Bay beach.

Closeby is the International Bar, which is more local than international, and is sometimes used on Sunday mornings for Catholic services. Beyond this area, known as La Pomp, is Paget Farm. Different from any other part of the island, it is isolated by its rude terrain, its torturous, busted-up road, and the independence of its people, who tend to keep to themselves.

Paget Farm is sparse with little rainfall. Fishing sailboats, painted in vivid reds, blues, greens and yellows dominate the rugged, stoney beaches. There are a few shops on the sea side of the road, selling groceries, snacks and rum. On the land side of the road you find weathered gray houses, a small Anglican Church which badly needs painting, and an overgrown cemetery, with markers dating back to the 1800s. Father Ron Armstrong, a Canadian, who retired in 1980, is minister of the Anglican Church. In an area that is about a mile long and a few hundred yards wide, there are ten churches, including Save Soul, Long Dress, God is the Answer, Church of God, as well as the more conventional denominations such as Anglican, Baptist, and Seven Day Adventists. Long Dress is probably the most unique. The female members of the Church wear long dresses at all times, even when bathing. Their ritual is similar to the Shakers, with much shaking, trembling, and dancing.

Beyond Paget is a stone quarry and a path along the water's edge at the base of steep volcanic cliffs that leads ultimately to Moonhole, where Tom Johnston, an ex-advertising executive, built his home inside a horizontal crater in the side of a mountain, through which you can see the Atlantic to the east and the Caribbean to the west.

Nice things kind of happen spontaneously on the island. I remember that I was walking along the beach in the direction of the Frangipani, when I heard someone singing, accompanied by a piano. It was my first visit to Bequia and I had been told that there were no pianos on the island. I quickened my step to find the origin of the music. This was my first introduction to the Frangipani. Inside, in the living room were two men, a bespectacled man in his sixties at the piano and a younger man, with a dimpled Irish face, singing a very moving Irish ballad. The piano player turned out to be Sandy Meisner, and the singer was Jimmy Carville, a Julliard graduate, whose main purpose at this point in his life was to teach the children of Bequia to sing like birds. It was a magical moment: Jimmy's fine tenor voice, Sandy's playing, and the sounds of the sea in the background. It was special. And that is the way Bequia is.

Bequia is special in different ways. For some it has been a turning point in their lives. It has had that kind of meaning for Tom and Gladys Johnston and Ron and June Armstrong and Jimmy Carville. For Violet and Rolf Wallach it has been a window to a world that is simpler, more carefree and less troubled than the one outside. For others, like Sandy Meisner, it is a place to recharge your batteries. For whalers like Athneal Ollivierre, it is the last place in the western hemisphere where whaling exists. For Nobleman, he looked homeward and found Bequia.

It spins its web in so many ways. Its magic is hard to analyze. But it is there. You can see the results.

MOONHOLE

All kinds of people have come to Bequia. Some have stayed for short periods, preferring the known to the unknown, the tried to the untried, the ordinary to the extraordinary. Others, like Tom Johnston and his wife, Glady, have made the island their home. The island has been their proving ground for smearing new ideas around, which Tom couldn't do very well back home without getting into trouble. They live at Moonhole, a very extraordinary creation.

You approach Moonhole by a path that runs from the stone quarry at Paget Farms to the bamboo entrance of Moonhole about a mile away. For about a third of the way the path follows the contours of the rugged steep cliffs at sea level and then passes through an open area of coconut trees, a boat wreck, and the remains of a sugar mill.

It is not an easy trek getting to Moonhole. When the tide is high, you are likely to get wet, and quite wet if the sea is angry. There is an alternate route, which is worse. The path leads up and down the steep hills. There have been plenty of times when people have just given up.

Moonhole is a very private place and so if you're planning a visit, it is best that you have a friend of the Johnston's make a telephone call in your behalf. The place isn't exactly impenetrable. If you are of the feminine gender and you run into Tom Johnston, he is just likely to drop whatever he is doing and graciously show you about. Glady, his wife, is not so easy to manipulate. There have been occasions when Glady has turned visitors away, always politely, only to run into them later in the company of Tom. She is more amused than distressed.

I don't want to give the impression that Glady is inhospitable. She isn't. She is just so busy running Moonhole that she has to plan her day tightly to get everything done. Tom is the creative member of the team and so is likely to have more time at his disposal. His day more or less develops as it goes along. He has a number of interests. He has built many free-form homes for his friends at Moonhole. He has developed his own art form which he calls scrim-sculpture. He is particularly interested in whaling.

Moonhole is a large hole, about 100 feet high and 75 feet wide, that nature has carved in the side of a hill. You can see through the hole from the Atlantic to the Caribbean. Tom created a free-form home in this crater that is different, dramatic, and to some a little weird. Nothing in the building is square. There are no windows or doors, just openings. The ceilings are at different levels and the walls go their own way independently.

27

The dining area, where Moonholers get together for parties and Sunday brunch, is typical Moonhole construction. High above the sea, you reach it by a series of steep winding stone steps. The room, if you can call it that, is about 35 feet long and irregularly shaped. The floors and walls are made of volcanic stone. There is no wall on the western side, just a large opening, the length of the room, with a breathtaking view of the Caribbean. In the center is a long free-form table, with a beautifully grained mahogany top, supported by stone pillars. Benches, also made of stone and made comfortable with pillows, flank the table. There are a few decorations, mostly samples of Tom's scrim-sculpture, which are etchings and carvings in whalebone. A path chiseled into the rock takes you down the cliff to the sea below. A heavy anchor chain, rescued from a boat, borders the path and provides protection. There is no beach below, just a jetty that protrudes into the sea. Tom's current project is building a free-form pool in the sea.

Tom tells the story about the time he was greeted by George Tannis, the tax assessor.

"I'm here to measure your house for tax purposes," Mr. Tannis said.

"Is your definition of a house a place with rooms?" Tom asked.

"Well, yes."

"A room is a place with four walls?"

"Of course."

"Then you are going to have trouble measuring this place," Tom said.

Tannis looked around. The house had many roofs, none

of them connected. It had many floors, at different levels. Also the floors were not connected. The walls were twisting, bulging, angling, anything but square. Only in a few places did they come together. It was impossible for Tannis to be able to tell where the non-taxable outdoors ended and the taxable indoors began.

Faced with an impossible situation, Tannis sighed and said, "Let's have a beer."

Tom has never had any architectural or engineering training. Yet he has successfully built more than a dozen homes, many of which have been written up in architectural magazines. "I'm like a Bequian boat builder," he says. "I never use plans. I wouldn't know what to do with them. I start with a pile of rocks and sand and cement. Don't tell me what you want. Let me build the house that I think you want. I start at a point and I follow the contours of the ground and the relevancy of the sky and the sea. I create a house. Once I get started, it moves along pretty quickly. If I don't like what I've done, I either knock it down, or hide it, if it isn't critical. Oh, I take instructions up to a point. You can tell me how many bedrooms and bathrooms you want, but don't tell me where they are to go. I have never had anyone tell me that they didn't like what I had done."

Sounds like a prima donna? Well, he is, but a good natured one, and to my knowledge no one has ever been offended by his attitude or displeased with the results.

You can operate the way Tom does when you have found your niche, and it fits, and it works for you. Tom is outgoing, gregarious, fun loving. The world, that being Moonhole, is truly his oyster.

29

Finding his niche, however, didn't come quickly or easily. It took Tom 50 years to find Moonhole and to realize that this was the answer to his search. If there is any word to describe Tom's growing up, his education, his short career in journalism and a longer one in advertising, that word is maverick. He is fun loving, unpredictable, impulsive, and sometimes outrageous. He prides himself that he got fired from practically every job he had ever held. He gets a kick out of talking about what might seem to be failures, but really weren't, because Tom proved a point each time and each firing was really an accomplishment because it led to something bigger and better. Tom loves to talk about himself, Moonhole, Bequia, his careers, and most important, Glady.

Tom looks like a leprechaun, an overgrown one. His eyes twinkle and he has a mischievous smile. He has a big loose frame and he gets around easily. Glady usually keeps his straight gray hair at a reasonable length, which is neither long nor short. He is very comfortable with people and just as comfortable alone. He has a studio where he disappears to. The studio is usually cluttered with scrim-sculpture in various stages of development. He won't let anyone in to clean up, so it is usually in a state of serious disarray.

Glady is different. She is small, petite, neat. She is loaded with energy and always on the go. She has a full time job running Moonhole. She supplies all of the maids and the food that the maids prepare. Her canteen is bigger than many of the markets on Bequia.

In the beginning Moonhole was run like a very sophisticated kibbutz. The original group of owners was very close. They had all their meals together. They were important people from different fields and their discourses were lively and productive. In time the closeness became too much and the communal spirit disappeared. Today, only Sunday lunch is communal and for the most part people at Moonhole go their independent ways.

One time I asked Glady what Moonhole meant to them. She said, "We have grown closer. Moonhole has helped to release our natural rivalry. We have greater respect for one another, we're kinder, care more. Nothing has happened to our essential differences. We've learned to handle them better."

I thought that was quite a statement at the time. I still do.

It seems that Tom has always traveled along an unconventional path. For example, when he was sixteen he applied for admission to Deerfield Academy in Massachusetts to be near his sweetheart. The fact that he got turned down didn't matter. He went there anyway. He attended classes and hid out in the infirmary. Three weeks later the headmaster recognized him as a rejection. Johnston said, "I always heard you never let a real problem boy go, and I am certainly a problem." He was allowed to stay, provided that he agreed not to return the following year. Contrary to his word, he returned, graduated from Deerfield, and a year later applied to Princeton. He failed the entrance exam and then attended Huns School which specialized in getting academic delinquents into Princeton. Eventually, he entered Princeton, and got his letter at wrestling, football, and lacrosse.

Tom emerged from Princeton in 1933 without a diploma. "That was due to two things," Tom explained. "First, I was a mediocre student. Second, in my senior year, I wrote a paper claiming that Melville was a better writer than Hawthorne, who I said was a dumbbell. That didn't sit well with the faculty.''

He had several tours with the Furness Line while at Princeton and traveled about the Caribbean. On one tour the boat stopped at St. Vincent. Tom made note that one day he would return to the island.

Tom made his debut in the advertising field in 1936. A buddy of his told him about an opening with J. Sterling Ketchel and he got an appointment with Ketchel. ''That was some interview,'' Tom said. ''He told me how to grill a fabulous steak and I told him how to grill a fabulous chicken. Suddenly he jumps out of his chair, remembering an appointment out of the office. He rushes out of the office to the elevator and I follow him. As the elevator door closes, he shouts back to me, ''You're hired!'' I learned later that Ketchel had told his staff that if a truck driver had showed up, he would have hired him. Ketchel said, ''I'm so goddamn sick and tired of those English majors from the Ivy League!''

Tom stayed with Ketchel to 1939, then moved on to BBD&O. ''I wrote trade advertising for U.S. Steel, Ethyl, and others. Trade advertising stank. It was done by cub writers. The better writers wouldn't stoop to trade writing. I wrote a memo to all account executives. I said I would eat any trade advertising run in the past two years, if I couldn't do better.''

The result of that memo was that Tom got fired. ''They were retrenching at the time and I would have gotten fired anyhow with several hundred others,'' he explained.

''I had saved $3000 by this time and I decided to go on

a cruise in the Caribbean with my wife!''

"I thought you married Glady after the war," I said.

"This was my first wife," Tom said.

"I didn't know."

"She was my childhood sweetheart, the one I went to Deerfield to be near."

Tom looked away. His usual bounce was gone. He looked sad.

I felt uncomfortable and said, "You'd rather not talk about it."

"It's okay," he said. "I don't talk about that part of my life very much. Maybe I should." He composed himself quickly. "She went to Smith and I went to Deerfield. Her mother was Isabel Cabot, who couldn't stand me and I couldn't stand her. She wanted better for her daughter, which wouldn't have been difficult. She sent her daughter away to Europe to complete her education. That was the summer of 1933. We didn't see one another until 1936. I was in Southern Pines, where I was born. I remember getting all dolled up for the ball. I love hunt balls. They're like something out of the past. Well, there she was on the dance floor. I cut in. She told me her partner was her fiance. I said he had been. We had a fabulous courtship and a fabulous marriage. She died in 1942. Jim, my son, you know him, was a year old and Evelyn two and a half."

Tom stopped cold at that point. He didn't mention his wife's name or the cause of death.

I felt I had trespassed enough and remained quiet.

"During the trip we stopped at St. Vincent," Tom said. "It was very colonial. We hobnobbed with the gentry, the

Hazells, Punnets, and Childes. It was fabulous. I loved it.''
I noticed he was back to the singular tense. "Stayed until
the $3000 ran out which took damn near a year.''

"I left something out," Tom said. "I worked briefly
for McCann Erickson after I got fired from BBD&O. I went
back to McCann Erickson when I returned, stayed for a year
until the war broke out. I joined the War Production Board
and in 1942 enlisted in the Navy. I was in the amphibious
forces in both the Atlantic and Pacific theatres.''

When the war was over, he returned to Southern Pines,
North Carolina, where he had grown up. Catherine Byrd,
a widow of a close friend of Tom's, Jim Byrd, published
a weekly newspaper, the Sand Hill Pilot.

"She invited me to join the newspaper as associate editor,
which I accepted," Tom said. "I was left in charge of the
newspaper when she went away to Jackson Hole on vacation.
I had a ball. I played hell with the local politicos. They were
involved in all kinds of minor chicanery. You couldn't get
anything done with the police unless you bribed them with
a bottle of liquor. I wrote humorous articles about the police.
They threatened me. I threatened them back. I said to them,
'You haven't got a leg to stand on and you know it. So why
are you bothering me?' Well, I succeeded in making myself
unpopular. People began to dislike me so much that when
I went to a football game, those around me would get up
and move to other seats.''

Finally, the town mugwumps, as Tom describes them,
had enough and the Mayor, the police chief and the head
of the American Legion sent a joint telegram to Mrs. Byrd
saying that he was ruining the newspaper.

34

"Catherine wrote to me ordering me to cease and desist. I responded by quitting. She calls me on the phone and prevails upon me to stay until she returns, which I did."

Tom returned to the advertising field at this point and re-joined McCann Erickson. While with that agency, he met Anderson Hewitt.

"We became great friends," Tom said. "I learned later that he was impressed with my boots. He said he knew I was a gentleman by my boots. I didn't have the heart to tell him I found them. Well, Hewitt starts an agency, Hewitt, Ogilvy, Benson and Mathers. That was in 1948. A year later they get the Sun Oil account and knowing my earlier experience in the oil field they ask me to join, which I did. I stayed with the agency until 1952. One day Ogilvy tells me it was the biggest mistake of his life when he let Hewitt become president. I reminded him that it was Hewitt's money and Hewitt's influence that enabled the company to get started and that he, David, was nothing. I said to Ogilvy. 'You will agree that you are a very smart man.' He agrees. 'I will give you two years and you will see what a two-faced sonnavabitch you really are. You won't have a friend left!' "

"You got fired," I said.

"No, to my surprise," Tom said. "That happened a little later. I was invited to talk at a luncheon meeting of advertising managers. I guess I got carried away a little. I said that advertising agency people thought that advertising managers had shit for brains. That appeared in Advertising Age."

Almost immediately thereafter Tom left the firm and joined Turner & Tyson. That was in 1954.

"I made one condition that they give me as many titles

as Jack Tinker had," he said and laughed. "Well, I couldn't afford to stay and again returned to McCann Erickson."

"Mother McCann," I said.

"You're right. I must have worked for them at least four or five times."

Tom began to reminisce about Marion Harper, the boy wonder in the advertising field, who became president of McCann Erickson at the age of 28.

"I remember when he joined the company as an office boy. He had a soft physical presence, but he was smart. He came up through market research. He came up fast and he fell fast. He's living on social security now with his mother in Oklahoma. He owes Uncle Sam so much in back taxes that there's no point in working. I feel sorry for him. Too damned smart."

"When I got fired by McCann in 1955, I was hired by Needham, Lewis & Brody in Chicago. That was the year I proposed to Glady. Oh, I forgot to tell you that we met in 1947. She worked for McCann in the research department. She was smart and had a damn good job. When I proposed to Glady she told me that I had twelve character flaws. She said I drank too much. That I talked too much. That I was always late. That I wasn't neat, and so on."

Glady joined us at that moment and listened to Tom reminisce.

"I told her I would deal with each character flaw, one at a time. So the first week, I was neat. The next I was punctual. I cut down on my drinking in the third. In the fourth I talked very little."

Glady chimed in. "How can you deal with a guy like

that? I couldn't, so I married him. Needless to say, he still has his character flaws, but I have learned how to deal with them, and they are less troublesome.''

Tom grinned impishly.

''I remember one time complaining to Tom about his lack of neatness,'' she said. ''He says to me, 'Why do you complain about my sloppiness? I don't complain about your neatness?' I think I realized then I was fighting a losing battle. Also that victory wouldn't be right for either of us.''

''After our marriage, I returned to Chicago with Glady. I was hired again by McCann Erickson, by Pete Peterson, who has had a fabulous career. He hired me as creative director. I told him to check it out with Marion Harper. He said that wasn't necessary. I told him he had better. Well, Peterson calls up Marion who is in a meeting, Marion takes the call anyway and when he learns what Peterson wants, he hangs up. Peterson calls again, and Marion hangs up. Each time he says no. Finally, on the third call, Harper says, 'Oh Christ, if Glady can put up with him, I guess we can too.' ''

Tom stayed with McCann for three years.

''I got what I wanted. Pete Peterson was the greatest guy in the marketing field at the time. I worked directly with him and I learned a hell of a lot. He had a guy in his office, Chet Posely, who I didn't like and unfortunately he became head of the Chicago office.''

The pattern repeated itself and again Tom quit McCann Erickson. Now he joined Draper, Daniel and Leo Burnett.

''Leo was the brains,'' Tom said. ''They were creative cannibals. A fabulous group. I thought I was making a big contribution. But then the inevitable day came. I had worked

37

all weekend on a Chrysler proposal. When I showed up Monday morning for the creative meeting, I found that the meeting was going full blast and that the group had already agreed on the campaign for which I was to be in charge. You can guess what happened.''

I didn't have to guess. But what I wasn't aware of was that Tom's house had burned down at the same time.

"Everything was totaled. That was 1959. I was fed up with advertising. I had turned fifty and decided there was something better that I could do with the next fifty years.''

"Enter Bequia,'' I said.

"Right. We went to Bequia on vacation and stayed at the Sunny Caribee. I became manager and Glady and I ran it together. Jerry Palmer had an interest in the company that owned the Sugar Mill in St. Vincent and the Sunny Caribee. He was an officious ass. I remember one day he came over from St. Vincent to make an inspection. He brought along his secretary. He went over the hotel, every inch of it, and as he made his inspection he dictated notes to his secretary as to what had to be done. When it was completed, I said to him, ''Well Jerry you've done my job for me. I quit.''

Jim, his son, didn't share his father's enthusiasm about moving to Bequia. "He really couldn't understand it or accept it,'' Tom said. "When he applied to Boulder College for admission, he had to indicate his father's occupation. He wrote 'plumbing inspector'.''

Tom and Glady learned that the area at the southwest end of the island was for sale and they bought it. That was to become Moonhole.

At long last Tom was to become involved in something

that belonged to him and Glady and where he could give vent to his creative impulses and no one existed who could fire him.

"Hallelujah," Tom exclaimed.

The non-conformist had finally found the milieu in which to non-conform.

"I think it is a matter of genes," Tom said. "My mother was a non-conformist. She was the first to ride astride in Madison Square Garden. She was disowned by her parents for showing her thighs. She went to Washington in search of a job. She learned quickly that men were better paid. So she masqueraded as a man. She called herself George Crawford. He maiden name was Agnes Crawford Gale. One day she was caught up with in the men's room by a man who later became my father."

I asked Tom and Glady where they intended to go from here.

"We have everything here we want but money. We don't need money. We are enjoying our lives. We have everything that money can't buy."

"I remember one of our early days at Moonhole," Glady said. "We have a photograph somewhere that shows me standing in the bedroom with a wan smile. We had no closets or shelves. Just boards across rocks. I tried to be gung-ho about the fact that the bedroom floor ended close to the bed and that there was nothing to keep me from falling out of the room. I remember Tom repeating, 'I know you are going to be happy! I know you are going to be happy!' until I really was."

"I love my life here," Tom said. "I'm creating something

all the time. It's like painting with your feet. I keep smearing ideas around."

In his houses you will find anchor chains as railings; whale-ribs and vertebrae as desk tops; deadeyes as towel racks; spars, masts and hatch covers as beams. He uses jetsam tastefully and always for practical purposes. Never just to create an atmosphere. There's a saying on Bequia, 'Don't throw anything away. Sell it to Tom Johnston.'

"I love to build," Tom says, "and I build only for friends. I am the lowest cost builder on the island, because I really don't care about making money. What I get out of it is a fabulous life. I've got Glady and my son, Jim, is working with us. I'm 77 and I've got another 10 years to create things that I like." He stopped for a moment and started on a new train of thought. "I am going to get interested in video taping. I am going to document whaling. I've talked to Athneal about this and he likes the idea."

Apparently there is no end to his stream of new ideas. Seventy seven years young.

DOWN TO THE SEA

The sea holds a deep fascination for Bequians. A psychologist might explain that with the end of slavery in 1838 the people were subconsciously in search of a new identity and they found it in the sea: in fishing, whaling, and boat building.

Bequia's claim as the last of the whaling islands may be short-lived. The only whaler-captain still operating on the island is Athneal Ollivierre, who has two boats, the Why Ask? and the Dart, each with a crew of six, which continue to ply the waters in search of the humpback whale. Considering his advancing age, and that none of the younger generation has shown much interest in whaling, the noble and romantic pursuit of the leviathans of the sea may soon become an extinct exercise in deering-do in this part of the world.

Recently I met Athneal on the beach at Friendship Bay as he and his crew dragged Why Ask? onto the beach. His eyes were bloodshot and he looked very fatigued. He knew why I was there and he invited me back to his house to continue our talk. We sat at the kitchen table and I looked around while he washed up. The kitchen was very plain, like the rest of the house. By American standards, the refrigerator and stove were antiques. There were two doors in the kitchen. One led to a storeroom where he kept his gear; the other to a bedroom where his wife, suffering from swollen ankles, was resting.

I brought a bottle of rum, which I put on the dining room table. Athneal reminded me that he did not drink but motioned me to fill a glass he had brought to the table for me. I studied him closely. He looked the part of a warrior. He was lean and you sensed great strength, particularly in his wrists and arms. He had a narrow, drawn face with deep set gray eyes, high cheekbones, and curly, closely cut hair that had begun to gray. His face was weathered and deeply lined. He had a very serious look about him.

"We had him, but we had to cut him loose," he said. "He would have taken the boat straight down." He talked some more about the day and his frustrations and then we got around to the subject I wanted to talk to him about, the future of whaling on Bequia. His gaze dropped to the floor and he looked sad. "It is not very good," he said. "I have eleven men and none is prepared to replace me when the time comes." "Why?" I asked. "It is a dangerous business. When I was sick last year and went to the hospital, the boats went out but they caught nothing." You could see that it pleased him that there was no one like Athneal with the required deering-do. He wasn't bragging. He was stating a simple fact.

"We had a real scare last year," he said. "We struck

a great big bull. Instead of fleeing, he turned, ran under us and lifted the boat clear out of the sea. One of the crew was very black. He turned absolutely white! He did! Believe me, he did!'' He laughed now for the first time since he came in. He began to relax, but he wouldn't join me when I poured another rum.

I asked him if he had ever seen the movie, 'Moby Dick.' ''That whale was just like Moby Dick,'' he said, ''a very mean, nasty fellow.'' It was fascinating to watch Athneal as he talked about whaling and the sea. His face was alive and his speech quick and he laughed. You felt his excitement and joy. I was going to ask him why at an age closing in on sixty he was still whaling. It really wasn't necessary. You could see that whaling was in his blood. It was his life and he would continue just as long as he possibly could.

A local historian, Inness Quashie, states in his book, *Whale Industry in Bequia,* that whaling began when the French settled there in the 17th and 18th centuries. It could have started earlier. It has been established that Basque whaling boats sailed in the Azores and other parts of the Atlantic in small fleets by the 15th century. The first recorded reference to whaling in the South Atlantic was in a report by Uriah Bunker of Nantucket in 1775 that he had discovered whaling grounds off South America. Since the Caribs were good sailors and fishermen, they may have pre-dated everyone else.

Whaling in the Atlantic and later in the Pacific became a big industry in the early 1800s. By the 1820s there were over 500 whaling vessels operating out of New England, with 15,000 sailors on board, and a catch valued at $10 million annually. According to John Edward Adams, Professor of Geography, University of Minnesota, vessels based in New England made regular cruises in Caribbean waters in search of sperm whale, humpbacks, and pilot whales. He states that the most popular hunting grounds extended from the Windward Islands to the northeastern coast of South America.

In 1868 the St. Vincent Bluebook, which is the country's official record of commerce and industry, noted that "American whaling vessels annually visit these islands and take large quantities of oil from the humpback and the blackfish (pilot whale)." Next year it stated, "In 1868 whale oil ranked 4th in the value of exports from St. Vincent, behind sugar, rum, and arrowroot, but ahead of cotton and molasses." From 1867 through 1870, according to the Bluebook, 6,702 barrels and casks of whale oil, amounting to over 250,000 gallons and valued at 28,000 pounds, were shipped from St. Vincent.

The first whaling company started operations in Bequia in 1875. It was organized by William Thomas Wallace II, son of the English naval lieutenant who came to Bequia in 1840. The Bluebook in 1876 noted, "There are now 3 or 4 whaling boats owned in the Grenadines which go out fishing in the channels between the islets." Wallace's whaling operation consisted of a shore station, with facilities for boiling oil from blubber, on the west coast of Friendship Bay. Sometime in the 1870s Joseph Ollivierre also erected a whaling station and located it on Petit Nevis, about a half mile offshore from Bequia, which was later abandoned in favor of a new site at Semple Cay, a low islet a short distance from Friendship Bay. Joseph Ollivierre's sons served as officers on the whaleboats and ran the station.

By now the Ollivierres and Wallaces and other families, the Sargeants, Kidds, and Hazells were very active in whaling, crewing on vessels from New England, as well as operating their own boats. The log of the William A. Grozier, which whaled out of New Bedford from 1888 to 1908, listed four Bequians — Ollivierre, Sargeant, Kidd and Hazell — as crew members. Their descendants are much in evidence in Bequia today, particularly the Ollivierres.

By 1890 there were six whaling fisheries operating in Bequia. Ten years later they provided employment for one third of the working male population of Paget and Friendship Bay. Whaling hit its zenith in the early 1900s and then started to decline in the 1920s when humpback whales became scarce as a result of excessive kills. Between 1949 and 1957 not a single whale was caught. In 1958 three were taken and since then a few have been caught most every year. Today, Bequia is the last island in the Caribbean engaged in whaling, and it has only two whaleboats in operation, the Why Ask? and the Dart, both owned and operated by Athneal Ollivierre.

Unlike in other seas, where whaling is slaughter on a grand scale, capture of three whales would be considered a successful year in Bequia. None has been caught thus far this year. The contest between the whale and the whaler distinctly favors the whale due to its speed and because the technology of whaling has progressed very little. The method and the implements of the hunt have not changed much over the years. The hunt is conducted in an open sailboat about twenty six feet long, powered by four oars, as well as the wind. The harpoon is handthrown and the kill is accomplished by lances that are thrust into the side of the whale. A whale gun, looking like a shortened blunderbuss, and weighing close to fifty pounds, is carried along but used only when other methods fail. It shoots a projectile about twelve inches long containing a charge which explodes after contact. One of the reasons it is not popular is the gory mess it creates.

The whaling season starts with the blessing of the whaleboats by Father Ron Armstrong late in January when humpbacks appear in the shallow bays, coastal shelves, and channels of the Grenadines. These are their breeding grounds. They mate here and ten months later they return to have their young. They begin the migration back to northern waters in March, their ultimate destinations being the feeding grounds off Maine, Newfoundland, Greenland and Iceland. The calves remain with their mothers for a little less than a year, the time required to make the round trip north and back. The humpbacks pass between Bequia and Mustique, nine miles away, as they migrate first south and several months later north. They usually migrate in families, a bull, a cow, and their offspring. The bull is the most difficult to catch. The cow is easier because she is protective of her calves. The usual technique is to catch one of the unsuspecting calves. The mother seeks to protect her offspring and in the process is frequently caught herself.

The scenario does not always happen that way. Most times the herd escapes for the simple reason that logistics favor the whales. They can move faster than a whaleboat and they can dive for periods as long as twenty minutes. The averages favor the whales, for while twenty sightings is normal in a season, a catch of three is considered good.

Whalers go out most every day in the whaling season

when weather conditions permit. They are guided by spotters on a hill who maintain a constant lookout for whales and communicate their location and direction of movement to whalers by mirrors. The system is called "using the glass." The boats also carry walkie-talkies but the messages are frequently garbled and the "glass" is considered more reliable, at least when the sun is out.

When a whale is caught, the entire island turns out in celebration. The parties go on until the butchering is completed and the last pound has been sold. There is much singing and dancing, steel bands perform, and rum flows freely, and yet the parties never get out of hand so as to cause a public disturbance that would get the local constabulary involved. Bequians have long learned that the best way of maintaining law and order is to keep the police out. Police only seem to contribute confusion and occasionally they hurt one another accidentally.

The butchering takes place on Petit Nevis, a small uninhabited island about a half mile offshore to the south of Bequia. Doing the grizzly work offshore is not so much a matter of protecting the sensibilities of the public, as a convenience. When the job is done, the remnants are simply washed out to sea, to the delight of waiting sharks.

The value of the catch is based entirely on the number of pounds of flesh that it will yield at the going rate of three E.C. dollars a pound (a little over a dollar in U.S. money). The days when whale oil was used for lighting, or when ambergris was used to produce perfumes are long gone. Whale teeth are still prized but for many years it was illegal in the States to traffic in whale teeth. Tom Johnston represents a ready market for whale bones which he uses in his scrim-sculpture. The total value of a whale runs about $25,000 in U.S. currency, which is split in eighteen shares, with each member of the crew of the two boats getting a share, the boats' owner two shares per boat, and the spotters a share each. The financial rewards are modest and for that reason all those engaged in whaling have other jobs out of the whaling season and there is no ready backup of potential whalers to succeed the present crews when they ultimately go into retirement. The Bequians' deeply rooted love for the sea is the only possible explanation for the fact that today there are still two whaleboats and twelve men, including Athneal Ollivierre, who continue to hunt the great leviathans.

Wherever there is a beach you are likely to find a boat being built. Most are double-enders, or two-bow boats as they are called locally. The smaller ones, 16 and 18 footers, are used for fishing. The whaleboats are larger, about 26 feet, and are very similar to the lines of the Nantucket and New Bedford whaleboats. They have a long shallow keel so that they can be dragged up on the beach and they use a great deal of ballast to keep them on point.

Bequians have developed the ability to build fairly large vessels, and they too are constructed either on a beach or on a slope next to a beach. The largest boat built on the island was the Gloria Colita, which was captained by Reg Mitchell, father of Son Mitchell, the Prime Minister. It was a three masted schooner, 165 feet long and it weighed 178 tons. Mitchell owned two schooners before building Gloria Colita. First was the Water Pearl, 94 feet long and 68 tons, which was built in partnership with his father and was launched in

1932. Two years later the schooner failed to come about when tacking off Bequia Head and was blown ashore. Next came the Juliana which Mitchell used as a freighter between British Guyana and Cuba.

The largest boat built since then is the Friendship Rose, about 115 feet in length. It was launched in 1969 and is used to carry people and freight between St. Vincent and Bequia. It operates like clockwork, leaving Bequia at 6:30 a.m. and returning at 1:45 p.m. It runs five days a week and never on Saturday since the captain is a Seventh Day Adventist and seldom on Sunday, which is a holiday, unless he can get a charter to Mustique. To my knowledge, it has never missed a day, which cannot be said of the other boats making the run between Bequia and St. Vincent.

All of the boats are built by sight, and not by plans. It is a skill that a number of Bequians have acquired. It usually runs in families, like the Mitchells, the Goodings, and the Simmons, and is passed down from generation to generation.

The launching of a schooner is a big event. Dozens of people may be involved in moving it from its site into the sea. Rollers are made from the trunks of coconut trees and the hull is guided down the slope to the beach by ropes fastened to the hull and secured to trees. Getting the boat into the sea is a slow and dangerous operation and usually takes the better part of a day to accomplish.

When the hull hits the sea and is secured, the inevitable party begins and it goes on and on through the rest of the day and the night and sometimes the next day until sheer exhaustion brings it to an end.

When the Mitchells a few years ago launched the Wave

Dancer, which was built on the side of a hill bordering Friendship Bay beach, hundreds came to Friendship Bay to celebrate. They danced, played cricket, swam, picnicked and, of course, drank rum. Steel drums could be heard as far away as La Pomp, guitarists played for small groups, and amateur singers took the opportunity to sing their own calypso ballads. Bequians love a party and this was a party.

An important source of income to the island is contract sailing. Many of the men regularly go to sea as sailors on cargo vessels for periods of a year and longer. When they come home (they always do), they have a nest egg and they spend it in one of three ways: building a home, buying a car to go into the taxi business, or starting some other kind of business.

Fishing is the island's main occupation and there is a particularly heavy concentration of fishermen on Paget Farm and La Pomp on the southside. The dominant names here are Ollivierre, Sargeant, Lewis, Kidd, and Hazell, the same names that appeared in the logs of whalers from New England a hundred and more years ago. The Kidds take pride in claiming that they are direct descendants of the notorious Captain Kidd.

As you might expect on an island that is oriented to the sea economically and emotionally, telling stories about the sea is a favorite way of passing time when there is nothing better to do. The usual spot is under the almond tree in the harbor. Another is the International Bar at La Pomp. Stories abound about the disappearance of boats at sea. Even in this remote part of the world, the Bermuda Triangle is known and discussed. There are stories about pirates still operating in the Caribbean. Smuggling is commonplace, and except for drugs most smuggling involves ordinary things, like cheese and wine from the French islands.

Several times I have heard the tale about the disappearance of Reginald Mitchell, father of the Prime Minister, near Cuba in World War II. His schooner, the 165 foot long Gloria Colita, was discovered foundering and awash in the open sea by a U.S. Coast Guard plane. The boat was deserted except for a dog. There was food on the captain's table, but the crew's quarters had been stripped clean. One story is that the crew had mutinied, killed the captain, and left in a rowboat, later to perish at sea. A more glamorous version is that the Colita was intercepted by a German U-boat, that Captain Mitchell was forced on board the U-boat to help pilot the submarine in local waters, and that the crew was put in a rowboat and sunk. Credence is lent to this version by tales of a U-boat being spotted from time to time with a black man on deck.

Tales of the sea can sometimes stretch one's imagination. Horace Beck, author of books on whaling and witchcraft, tells the story of a boat out of Grenada that was constantly in trouble until the crew decided that the problem with the boat was that it had no soul. The crew selected one of its members to be sacrificed, whose soul would be given to the boat. From that time on the vessel sailed without mishap, and the only question raised by the parents of the departed crew member was why their son had been selected. There was no question about the propriety of the deed and the police never became involved.

Obeah is the name given locally to a form of witchcraft,

which had its origins in Africa. In the days of slavery, the bush doctor was the center of activities. He made medicines from a variety of herbs that were useful in curing many diseases. He dealt with spiritual matters and he was an advisor on many things. The development of obeah was an outcome of the parties that slaves would hold after a hard day's work to keep alive their African heritage. They would sing to the beat of native drums, participate in "ring" parties, which involved dancing in a ring and telling "anancy" stories about spirits and goblins. The obeah doctor today, like his predecessor, the bush doctor, is a person of considerable influence.

Among some Bequians, the obeah doctor is consulted before the clinic's doctor in the case of illness. While many on the island say they have never seen a jumbie, which is a reincarnated spirit that can take the form of a human or an animal, most everyone says he knows of someone who has. Every house on Bequia has its windows bolted shut at night to ward off evil spirits. There's a small stone bridge on the road to Spring Plantation which is called Jumbie Bridge. It is called that because it is said that a jumbie by the name Friday lives beneath it. None of the plantation workers will walk over the bridge at night.

The supernatural and the sea are closely entwined. Before a boat is launched, it is blessed by a member of the clergy. There is also a standard ritual for the blessing of whaleboats and for driving evil spirits out of houses and boats and trees. You occasionally see an isolated tree that has been burned to the ground to rid it of an evil spirit that had taken possession of it.

WHALE HUNT

Athneal Ollivierre is one of four brothers descended from Joseph d'Ollivierre who came to Bequia from France in the late 1700s. The first few generations were involved in growing sugar cane. That industry went into the doldrums when slavery was abolished in 1838. At about that time whaling ships from New England became familiar sights throughout the Grenadines and they made frequent stops to pick up supplies and recruit local fishermen to crew. At first the Ollivierres seemed content to join up as crew, but in time they learned that riches were to be won not by crewing but by owning. They built their first boat on the beach at Friendship Bay around 1875, launching an operation that was to grow and in time to become a much needed supplier of employment and income to Bequia.

The whaling industry on Bequia grew steadily until the 1920s when humpback whales became scarce as a result of excessive kills. Between 1949 and 1957 not a single whale was caught. In 1958 three were taken and since then a few have been caught most every year. Today, Bequia is the last island in the Caribbean engaged in whaling and it has only two whaleboats still in operation, both owned by Athneal Ollivierre.

We were getting ready to go on a whale hunt. It was early morning. The sun was just breaking over the sea beyond Friendship. I studied Athneal closely. His face was deeply lined and weathered coarse. He was not a big man. Slight of build, actually, but his arms looked like they were fashioned from spring steel. His eyes were gray and deeply set, a sign that somewhere along the line his French forbears may have married a Carib. He belonged to the Seventh Day Adventists and so didn't drink or smoke and seldom cursed. His angular face glistened now from the spray of the sea.

The wind freshened and our whaleboat, leaving Friendship Bay, picked up speed, heeling over sharply as it cut through the choppy sea. It was making good time, in excess of ten knots, heading eastward into the early morning sun in the direction of Mustique, about seven miles away. The daily hunt was on for the humpback whales, which pass between Bequia and Mustique in mid-Winter and early Spring, first heading south to breed and then north to feed.

Athneal was coiling rope carefully in a large tub, the end of which was secured to a six foot harpoon in the bow of the boat. There were four rowers, a helmsman, Athneal and myself.

A few minutes earlier we had launched the boat and rowed it out into the waiting wind. We stowed the oars quickly and raised the mast and unfurled the sails and the boat lurched forward like a sprung tiger. We had nothing more to do at this moment but join the captain and the helmsman searching the sea for signs of the humpback whale.

Sightings were becoming less frequent. In the 1960s thirty or so sightings in a season were common and a catch of three made a good year. Now the sightings were down to twenty, last year three were caught, and so far this year the whalers have drawn a blank. I had mixed feelings about whaling. Catching a whale was important to the livelihood of Bequians and a catch of three certainly had no impact on its endangerment as a species. I would not say this to any of my Bequian friends, but deep inside of me I felt sympathy for the whale. It was only fair that an animal so magnificent, so noble, so trusting should rise above the meanness of man and survive as it has for millions of years. I wondered what the ultimate outcome would be. Would it survive, or would its flukes and fins become legs again and would it return to land, which it had left millions of years ago? Would it look like a hippopotamus, from which some say it originated? My mind wandered as the monotony of scanning the sea took over.

Athneal's eyes swept the sea in search of signs. He had a very determined look, like that of a bullfighter. If he were a bullfighter, he would be dressed in gold breeches and a red cape and a toreador cap, but he wouldn't be any more brave. He explained to me why he was the last of the harpoonists. "It has to be in your blood to be a whaler," he said. "It is not something that you learn. It is very dangerous, and you are either brave or a fool. I'm not sure which. I know

55

of no one who wants to take over when I quit. It's a hard way to make a living, so why do it? Why run the risks? For the glory? The challenge? Maybe if you're like me. I suppose you will say that I am not very smart. Perhaps you are right. A smart person would find something else to do. Tend the goats. Or collect coconuts. Or write, like you.'' He laughed. ''Don't take offense. I know writing is not the same as tending goats or collecting coconuts. I could not do any of those things. My father was a whaler and his father was a whaler. I am born to it. I really have no choice. Besides, I like it. I don't know of anything I would rather do. It's my way of making a living and I am too old to change.''

At that moment a flick of reflected sunlight from atop Mount Pleasant caught his attention. I followed his gaze to the top of the hill. ''They've spotted a whale,'' he said, reading the signals from shore. ''Almost due south coming from Canouan. It should pass close to Mustique to the east. About twenty minutes from now.''

Nothing much changes, I thought. The whalers before him used the ''glass'' to communicate. And they sailed in open sailboats just like this — twenty six feet long, exactly the same as the old Yankee whaleboats to the last detail. And they hunt with a hand-thrown harpoon. It's no wonder that most whales escape their predators.

Athneal stood in the bow, and I was directly behind him. He turned to face the helmsman at the stern and shouted orders over the sloshing sounds of the boat cutting through the sea. ''More starboard,'' he said. ''Head for Mustique.'' He turned to me, and said, ''If the whale keeps on his present course, we should meet him at Basil's Bar.'' I smiled at his

56

whimsy and he broke into a broad grin.

We stared in the direction of Mustique. The wind freshened and we braced ourselves. The helmsman worked the tiller back and forth against the sea to keep the boat on course. We had nothing to do but wait and watch and prepare ourselves for the strike.

"She blows!" an oarsman shouted and pointed about ten degrees to starboard.

All eyes focused on the point. We could see the belch of steam clearly. The whale was about a quarter of a mile away, headed due north.

"Keep the course!" Athneal shouted. "We'll come up behind him! Get ready men! Pull the tiller! Use the long oar!"

We were close-hauled and the cold stinging spray whipped over the open deck. Everyone was tense, ready. I could feel adrenalin pumping. In a matter of minutes, we would be close enough to launch a strike. I was exhilarated but I also felt a little queasy. I had many feelings and I couldn't sort them out.

The boat sliced through the frothy water. The whale sounded again and we kept on our course, saying nothing, watching the sea, oblivious to the wind screeching through the stays. We sailed in complete silence for what seemed a very long time. Suddenly the whale broke the surface a hundred yards ahead of us and to our port side. The helmsman shoved the steering oar to starboard, let out some sail, and the boat responded immediately. We were behind the whale, his blind spot, and we were moving up rapidly on his starboard side. We were moving faster than the unsuspecting whale. We were almost on top of it.

"Now!" shouted Athneal.

The mast was unstepped, dropped to the deck, and the sails furled. We quickly dipped the oars into the sea and began to row strongly, quietly, in complete unison. We came up on the whale quickly. We were so close we could reach out and touch the unsuspecting leviathan.

"Oars in!" Athneal shouted and we brought the oars against the side of the boat. He stood with his legs braced against the gunnels, raising the six foot harpoon above his head in readiness. He was turned slightly to the port side. I could see him clearly. He had a wild, angry look on his face. He gritted his teeth, grunted, and flung the harpoon with a mighty trust into the side of the whale. Immediately the whale responded, taking off like a shot. The crew reacted with a mighty shout of approval.

"You stuck him good, real good!" I said.

"Mon, he's a big un!" the first oarsman exclaimed. "Fifty feet. Maybe sixty!"

Athneal was too busy to respond. The whale moved rapidly, dragging the whaleboat behind it. Athneal let out line from the big wooden barrel. All of a sudden the line went limp. The boat glided to a halt.

"He's coming back!", Athneal exclaimed.

Athneal brought in the line as fast as he could, not bothering to coil it, just dumping it in the tub.

The whale circled and then came straight at the boat from the port side. A hundred feet away it sounded.

We rowed in near panic, pulling as hard and as fast as we could to get out of its way. Everyone was shouting. We tried to get the cadence back. No way. We were stunned.

It was like being stuck on a railroad track with a huge loco-motive bearing down on us.

It happened quickly. The huge black, churning body dove under the boat and lifted it clean out of the water. For a very brief moment the boat was perched on its back. The whale shook and the boat nearly came apart. Not a sound was uttered by the men. We were too stunned to do anything to save our-selves. We sat rigidly for what seemed like a long time. The whale's flukes were out of water. One swipe and it would all be over. The whale shook again and the boat groaned and then the whale slipped below the surface and the boat slid off its back and dumped into the sea. The men grabbed at anything stationary to keep from falling into the sea. The boat heeled over sharply and then righted itself and settled down.

"Lord, oh Lord, oh Lord! " someone exclaimed.

There wasn't enough time to compose ourselves. The whale had turned and was running, dragging the boat behind it. Gradually the daze wore off and we were able to collect our senses. Athneal was still standing in the bow, holding on to the line, giving it up reluctantly to the whale.

"We still got him!" he shouted. "He can't shake it loose!"

"Let's give it up," the first oarsman said.

"That's enough for me," the second oarsman said.

"We're going to get him!" Athneal responded. "We're going to kill him!"

The crew fell silent and they looked at one another for answers.

"He damned near killed us!" Athneal shouted.

59

I had never seen him look like this. He was very angry. The muscles in his face and neck twitched. His face was wet with perspiration.

"We have no choice," he said.

The dimensions of the contest suddenly became apparent. We were in a death struggle for survival as Athneal saw it. If we didn't kill the whale, it would kill us.

"I say cut it loose," one of the rowers said.

"He will turn on us again," Athneal said, "and this time he will destroy the boat and us. We must get him first."

No one agreed but no one was prepared to confront Athneal.

The whale surfaced just ahead. It was moving slowly away. Athneal brought in the slack rope.

"Oars!" he commanded. Obediently we responded and quickly and quietly we pulled up behind the whale and now alongside it. Athneal had a seven foot lance in readiness. As we came alongside he flung it into the side of the whale, attempting to pierce the flesh between its ribs in search of the heart. The whale came alive. It shook violently and slapped the sea with its flukes, narrowly missing the boat, and then it dove into the sea.

"He's going deep!" Athneal shouted, paying out the rope.

We were being pulled along at a rapid clip. The bow of the boat dipped and the stern was slightly out of the sea, as the whale dove deeper and deeper.

"He's trying to take us with him!" Athneal said, giving up rope reluctantly. I reckoned that there couldn't be much rope left in the barrel.

60

There was nothing to do but sit and wait and hope that the whale would reverse his dive and come to the surface for air. Like a giant snake, the rope slid out of the barrel, through Athneal's hands and into the sea. We waited and waited and then suddenly the bow jerked deeper into the sea as the rope secured to a cleat in the bow came to an end.

"Cut it loose," someone shouted.

You could feel the boat strain to stay afloat. The bow was almost below the surface. The boat would either break up or go under, I thought.

"He's been down twenty minutes! He can't stand much more!" Athneal responded.

The boat was solid and heavy and strong, like all Bequia-built boats, but how much punishment could it take? It groaned as it sloshed deeper into the sea. It too was part of the struggle to survive. It held together bravely against the enormous force wanting to take it down to the bottom of the sea. All of a sudden the bow sprung from the sea like an uncaged tiger and the stern hit the sea with a thud.

"He's coming up!" Athneal shouted, elated. He rapidly hauled the rope back into the boat.

"That was too damned close," I said.

"But we beat him!"

I was flooded with a feeling of relief. I looked at the rest of the crew. They were hunched over, tired, fatigued. I was sure they would gladly give up the battle, if they had a choice.

"He'll be tired when he breaks the surface for air!" Athneal exclaimed.

We began rowing and Athneal pulled the rope in and

61

dumped it in the barrel. The whale surfaced dead ahead. My arms and shoulders and back ached and the cold spray stung my face and my lips felt raw. We cut through the waves like a knife. We were gaining on the lumbering, tiring whale.

We came up quickly alongside the whale. Athneal left the bow and came back to the bench where I was sitting. He climbed up on the bench, holding my head to steady himself. He placed one foot on the gunnel, waited, and then without a word leaped out of the boat on top of the whale, grabbed the lance stuck in its side and with all the strength he could summon he drove it deep into the whale's body. The whale shook like a locomotive off its track and then dove, leaving Athneal awash in the angry sea.

"A hand!" he shouted and suddenly the stunned crew came to life. They fished him out of the sea and brought him safely on board.

"Je-sus!"

Athneal was back on his feet in the bow of the boat.

"I got him good!" he hollered.

"You damned near killed yourself!" I responded.

I still couldn't believe what I had seen. It was preposterous. Did he think he was superman? Indestructible? For what?

Athneal said, as though he had read my mind, "It was our only chance. He would have come back at us again and he would have smashed us to pieces. Now, he is dying and we are alive."

The line slackened and the whale came to the surface. He was dying, I thought, or already dead. I remembered how exhilarated I had felt at the beginning of the hunt. Now I was tired and cold and I hurt all over.

The whale was motionless. We pulled up alongside him. He was dead. We rowed the boat around to the whale's head and two of the crew got out of the boat, climbing onto the whale and quickly sewed its mouth shut to keep it from taking water on the way back. The whale was secured to the stern of the boat, the mast stepped, the sails hoisted, and in a very short time we were on our way to Petit Nevis, a small island about a quarter of a mile offshore Bequia where the whale would be butchered.

With twenty-five or more tons of whale in tow, we moved slowly, tediously. By the time we reached shore, word had spread and a number of Bequians had already sailed over to help in the butchering and to party. Tired, we sat down on the beach next to a fire that someone had started. The heat from the fire felt good. We were wet and chilled and dusk was upon us and night would fall very quickly. One of the fishermen from Paget brought over a bottle of rum. I took a swallow, then two, and a third. Athneal declined. Another fisherman brought over a cup of coffee which he quickly accepted.

I was beginning to recover from what had been an overwhelming experience. I looked over at Athneal. Anger had disappeared from his face. He looked quite calm and collected. He noticed that I was staring at him and he smiled.

"Well, tell me, Tom, do you have any new thoughts about whaling?" he asked.

A lot of thoughts were racing through my mind but I was having difficulty putting them together coherently. It had been an exhilarating experience and a frightening one.

"If you're planning to go out again tomorrow, don't wait

for me," I said.

Athneal laughed.

People began gathering around us. Athneal was at center stage. He smiled, laughed, exchanged jokes with his admirers. He was the picture of a man who had triumphed over very great odds. He was sure of himself, composed, satisfied, very happy.

I began to see him in a clear light. A victor. A superb victor. The whale for all its size and strength and cunning and vengeance was no match for Athneal. Oddly, I did not feel sorry for the whale.

"He was a mean one, Tom, but we won."

I could think of no other place in the world but Bequia where Athneal could live out his life on his terms.

SANFORD MEISNER

(From Notables in the American Theatre.)

MEISNER, SANFORD. Teacher, actor, director. . . .Graduate Damrosch Inst. of Music (Now Julliard School of Music). . .Joined staff of Neighborhood Playhouse in 1935 and became head of the school in 1936. Remained head until 1959, when he resigned to teach privately in Los Angeles, and to direct the new talent division of 20th Century Fox; headed the dept. of drama for the American Musical Theatre Academy (1962-64); and returned to his former position as head of the Neighborhood Playhouse School. Between 1924 and 1938 he played in thirty one productions, including They Knew What They Wanted, the House of Connelly, Night Over Taos, Awake and Sing, Waiting for Lefty, Golden Boy, Rocket to the Moon, Night Music, Crime and Punishment. He also directed Waiting for Lefty, The Criminals, the Playboy of Newark, and The Time of Your Life.

Obviously, a man of substantial accomplishment and yet on Bequia he has described himself as being very plain, as plain as the paint on the wall. The contradiction whetted my interest. When I had the opportunity to sit in on one of his drama classes on Bequia, I gladly accepted. This was the third year that Sandy had invited groups of talented aspiring actors and actresses to come to this remote but lovely island in the Grenadines to participate in his drama workshop.

The program had expanded since it was started in 1985 on a trial basis. This past Spring he invited three groups of fifteen to twenty students to attend his workshop. The study program ran for a month, six days a week, from 10 a.m. to 5 p.m. There was a break of two weeks between each group. The program usually ended in mid-September, when Sandy was due back at the Neighborhood Playhouse in New York.

I was given a seat next to Sandy. We were in a large room in his home. There were fourteen students seated at one end of the room. The opposite end was raised like a stage with a door. Sandy sat at right angle to the students. With a slight turn of his head, he could face either the students or the stage. Sandy had aged since I first met him fifteen years ago. He seemed frail and smaller and he looked his age of 82. He had had a series of mishaps that would have undone most people. He went blind in one eye and lost his voice box to cancer in 1978. He had to use an amplifier to be heard in class. The device consisted of a small mike fastened to his glasses, with a cord that led to a transmitter in his shirt pocket. The words that he formed by belching gusts of air were transmitted to an amplifier in the middle of the room. Even so you had to strain to make out the words that he delivered in a slow halting monotone.

A young, pretty girl rose from her seat and approached the stage, followed by a young man. They faced Sandy and stood still, waiting for him to start. They were about to play a scene from Pygmalion. She was Lisa, the flower girl who Henry Higgins had brought into his home and changed from a cockney to a woman of breeding, who could pass herself off as such in any social situation. Henry Higgins had won his bet and now was no longer interested in the girl.

"What do you imagine your emotional condition to be?" Sandy asked the girl.

"I think I am furious with him. I am lost and I am very upset," she replied.

"Why is that?"

"Because all along I have been trying to live and learn with him. He never gave a second thought to what would happen after the task was done. And now all of a sudden, since the bet has been won, I have nowhere to go. All that he seems to care about is the bet, and not me. He's made a lady out of me but he treats me like a girl from the gutter," she said.

She looked at Sandy and waited for him to respond. He spoke slowly.

"Suppose that somebody had been using you and you heard the director say, 'Thank God we are rid of her!' Would that have an effect on you?"

"Yes."

"Well, you have to prepare youself. What do you think you have to prepare for?"

"The feeling of being used. Of being thrown away like trash."

"Yes, the feeling of being thrown away. Sit in the corner and prepare yourself."

We waited for her to prepare herself, to work herself into the proper emotional state. My mind drifted back to when I had first met Sandy. That was at the Frangipani. He was playing the piano and Jimmy Carville was singing a beautiful Irish ballad. They worked well together, I thought at the time. I wasn't surprised when I learned later that they had worked together for many years in the theatre in New York.

Sandy got his start in the theatre when he was seventeen. He played a bit part in the Theatre Guild production, "They Knew What They Wanted" in 1924. Through Aaron Copeland, who was a neighbor of Sandy's in Brooklyn, he met Harold Clurman and Lee Strasberg. I remember Sandy describing that experience.

"We worked in a settlement house on Christie Street," Sandy said. "It was an evening drama club, ladies from the International League of Garment Workers and men from the fur business. I always wanted to be an actor. When I was in 1A the teacher asked everyone in the class what they wanted to be. I said, an actor. Someone once asked me why I wanted to be an actor. I replied, 'If you ask Horowitz why he plays the piano, he would roll over on the floor with laughter."

"I won't ask that question," I said.

"I enjoyed acting but I didn't like being an actor. It made me too self-centered. I don't like that. It made me less of a person. There's something childish about being an actor. I don't deny that part of me is very much there, but it seemed to throw me off balance. It's different when I am teaching. I am working with objectives and I feel strong and my life healthier. The best of me comes alive when I am teaching."

I remember the occasion of our discussion. He and Jimmy had just finished putting on Jesus Christ Superstar and we were back at his home, relaxing with a drink. Sandy was tuned in to his past and he wanted to reminisce.

"The biggest influence in my life was Strasberg," Sandy said. "The fact that we went in different directions, well, that's life. I think my approach is healthier than his. He takes an introverted person and introverts him further. I always try to encourage truthful behavior relative to a situation. All of my theatrical exercises are designed to strengthen the guiding principle that I learned in the Group — that art expresses human experience truthfully."

Sandy was referring to the Group Theatre, which he had helped to found in 1930, along with Harold Clurman, Lee Strasberg, Stella Adler, Morris Carnovsky, Elia Kazan, John Garfield and others. I asked him about the Group.

"Being part of the Group Theatre was being part of a real theatre, where you worked in a serious way, in depth, and had the opportunity to develop your capabilities. It was the difference between being in show business and being in a real theatre. It was the place where I began to develop my talents as an actor and later as a director. One of the objectives of the Group was to do plays that had to do with the meaning of contemporary life. We were a company of actors, directors, and writers developing an art form that spoke to America, not country club America, but the tenements of the Bronx. We were part of the mainstream of America in the thirties."

Sandy lit a cigarette and poured another vodka and water.

69

He had not developed cancer as yet and spoke easily and quickly.

"Over the years of my work as a teacher, my standards and values as far as acting is concerned have remained the standards and values that were formulated by Stanislavsky and followed by the Group Theatre," he said. "If it weren't for the Group Theatre, I think I would still be in my father's fur business."

"How long were you with the Group?" I asked.

"Until it folded around 1940, Sandy replied. "I joined the Neighborhood Playhouse a few years earlier—in 1935—and I have been with the Playhouse ever since, except for a couple of years when I taught at Twentieth Century Fox. I've been with the Playhouse over fifty years. A lot of my students have become famous—Joanne Woodward, Eli Wallach, Tony Randall, Franchot Tone, Gregory Peck, John Voight, Steve McQueen.

It was getting late in the evening, but Sandy did not seem at all tired. It was obvious that he was enjoying the chance to rummage through the past.

"What is it about teaching that attracts you?" I asked. "You could have continued with acting, if you wanted to."

"I feel alive when I am teaching," he said. "I get an emotional release from it. This evening we did Superstar, Jimmy and I. I was involved in teaching and directing. I also played the piano. It was an exciting experience. Particularly doing it on Bequia."

Sandy had gone through several changes since I met him in the early seventies. He was physically strong and active in the beginning. Then there was a series of ailments and tragedies all bunched together around 1978. In addition to losing his sight in one eye and his voice box and getting hit by a truck in New York, he lost a very close friend, Paul Morrison, who was director of the Playhouse. Sandy was disturbed and numbed by the losses and he became more dependent on others, like Jimmy. That lasted until about three years ago when he began the drama workshop program on Bequia. With the workshop, he is busy six months of the year on Bequia, and back in New York he has the Neighborhood Playhouse where he continues in charge of the drama department.

My thoughts were brought quickly back to the present as Marjorie, playing the role of Liza in Pygmalion, rose to her feet and came to the center of the stage.

"Are you prepared?" Sandy asked.

"Yes."

"There's no scene unless you feel like a piece of junk that has been thrown out of the window. Now as a human being you have to translate that idea to emotional terms. How do you feel? You are broken hearted, right?"

"Right."

"Tell me how you have been misused."

"I have been treated like an experiment."

"And now you are finished. How do you feel about that?"

"Lousy."

Sandy did not respond immediately. He looked displeased. He gritted his teeth and looked down at the floor for what seemed a long time.

"You are not prepared," he shouted as best he could

sucking air through the hole in his neck. "You have got to learn to feel. You will never make an actress."

"That's not true!"

"You can't say that," Sandy said.

"I have to."

"No you don't have to. Nobody asked you anyway." Marjorie dropped to the floor and began to sob.

"I need to."

"You can get a job."

"I can't."

"You can get a job in Macys."

"I can't."

"Sure you can. That's what you are going to do."

"I won't."

"Go ahead. Let it out."

Marjorie was on her knees. She beat on the floor with her fists. She was crying profusely. She was not acting now. She was truly distraught.

Sandy motioned for Henry Higgins to enter. When Liza Dolittle saw Henry Higgins enter, she jumped to her feet.

"Where are my slippers?" he asked.

She picked them up and threw them at him.

"There!" she shouted.

"What's the matter? Did something go wrong?"

"I won your bet for you," she screamed at him. "Now I don't matter. What's to become of me?"

"How do I know what's to become of you. What does it matter?"

"What does it matter?" she shouted back. "You don't care. You wouldn't care if I was dead. I mean nothing to you."

And the play went on. The scene ended when Henry Higgins said he was tired and going to bed. They turned to face Sandy who looked down on the floor, then up at them, and back to the floor. Finally he spoke.

"If you don't work, if you don't prepare yourself, you cannot act," he said. "A few days ago you did act and it was surprising. It was so right the way you played off each other. It was a reliable performance. You allowed yourselves to behave spontaneously. I thought it was quite remarkable. You were right on the nose. Your acting was simple and honest. Now today you were unsure of yourselves. You hadn't worked obviously."

"You told me I could never be an actress," Marjorie said. "And that I would end up working in Macy's."

"I thought that imaginary example would devastate you. Right?"

"Right."

"It would bring to the surface the emotions you need. Do you follow?"

"Yes," she said. "So when I prepare for the scene I should feel the way you made me feel."

"You had difficulty emotionalizing yourself as a piece of trash," he said. "It all comes down to this, being yourself, effortlessly. You can easily learn to bathe. There's no effort. Acting must be the same. What you do, what you say, how you listen, how your hands work, when it is spontaneous, your emotions will come to the surface and what you say and do will be true. The key is that you must be yourself under circumstances that are imaginary."

73

I was on the edge of my chair throughout the performance. Sandy had worked them very hard. I had had no idea how demanding and relentless he could be. They must be exhausted, Sandy and the actors, I thought.

The workshop stopped for lunch and we went out on the terrace. I asked one of the students if the session was unusual.

"It happens every day and after a month of it we're emotionally ready to handle whatever comes up," he said.

I moved to the table in the dining room where Sandy and Jimmy were sitting. The room was dominated by a large armoire dulled by the effect of constant wind. In the corner was a pine hutch, with greeting cards stuck into the frame.

"He's changed," Jimmy said about Sandy. "He's gotten tougher, like he used to be. Joanne Woodward says he is as tough now as he was when she studied with him. He's quit smoking. Maybe that has something to do with it."

I asked Sandy why he had come to Bequia.

"I thought I was going to retire and that I would spend the rest of my life here on this beautiful island, living quietly. That was a mistake. Thinking I could retire. I need things to do. If I didn't have the drama workshop here, I would be stagnant. I can't read, except poorly out of one eye and I need Jimmy to read to me. And I speak the way you hear me. I can't swim anymore because of the hole in my throat. I could easily drown. So I am quite limited. I think I would die if I didn't have my workshop. The theatre is my life. Acting is like any other creative profession. An artist, a real artist, not the fakes, looks at a flower and he thinks from his true feeling about the flower. It is the same for an actor. He sees life truthfully and he projects it that way if he is any good.''

After what had to be an exhausting day, he looked alive and refreshed, much younger than in the morning, when I thought he looked his eighty two years of age.

BEQUIA REGATTA

The biggest event of the year on Bequia is the Easter Regatta, which starts Friday morning with the ocean-going yacht races and concludes Sunday afternoon when prizes are awarded. Everyone you know is likely to be there, either as contestants or as observers. It attracts people from the other islands, particularly St. Vincent. Last year three freighters brought over several hundred Vincentians who came with their own steel bands. They partied without a break for three days.

Yachts from the other islands and from Europe, Canada, and the United States compete in races around the island, a distance of about 30 miles, through seas that test the most experienced sailors. From the Bequians point of view, the major events are the races among the fishermen's sailboats and the two remaining whaleboats. They race from the Frangipani beach, around Moonhole, to Friendship Bay, and back, a run of about 15 miles.

Preparation for the Regatta starts months in advance of Easter. Sponsor of the event is the Bequia Yacht Club, which has a commodore and a vice commodore, just like any yacht club back home. The club does not have a yacht basin or a clubhouse and the members usually meet at the Frangipani. Workhorse of the club is Ellen Schwarz, who lives most of the year on her boat in the harbor and creates lovely scrimshaw pieces, which are sold in several of the gift shops. Twelve months of the year is too much paradise for most people, so she manages to go home to visit her family twice a year.

Ellen was responsible for the Bequia Regatta shirts that suddenly appeared all over the island. She ordered the shirts from Hong Kong, had them silkscreened on Bequia, and organized a sales staff to sell the shirts at the Frangipani. There was no way in the world that a passerby could avoid the display of T-shirts. Ellen also put together a souvenir program and no merchant on Bequia and St. Vincent was missed in her canvass of eligible sponsors.

One of the big supporters of the Regatta is the Prime Minister. His hotel, the Frangipani, serves as the unofficial headquarters for the Regatta. He is also involved as the official starter of the races and the awarder of prizes.

Last year the races of the fishermen's sailboats and the whaleboats were held on Saturday. The owners beached their boats near the Frangipani. The early birds got the best positions. What made certain positions better than others is hard to say. But the first ones placed their craft on the end of the beach closest to the Frangipani. Since the first leg involved

77

a course to port, perhaps that gave them an advantage of a few yards. Country Girl was one of the first to be beached and turned 180 degrees so that her stern was on the beach. She was the favorite in her class of 21 feet and had won every race in her class since it was launched in 1963. It would be sailed by Donovan Ollivierre, a big man with a deep bass voice, who makes his livelihood by going to sea on contract and between contracts by operating a taxi in the tourist season and fishing other times. He was very busy getting his boat in shape. He washed it several times, checked the sails, and coiled the ropes neatly. Pikie, nickname for Kennard Davis, was also busy with his boat, which had never won in its 18 foot class. Nobleman, who has sailed all over the world on contract and has logged more time as a commercial sailor than most others on the island, was on the scene. He didn't have a boat and was quite content to saunter along the beach occasionally and offer his approval or disapproval of a contestant's readiness. Nobleman had lived in England for 18 years and had played a trumpet professionally, which perhaps explained why he seemed different from most of his peers. He loves to get into conversations and he uses the word "exactly" often to underline his agreement. He is gentle and well-mannered and yet he has an impish side as well.

The crowds began to collect on the beach and on the Frangipani terrace, which provided the best views of the thirty five boats on the beach, bows to the sea, ready to start. The merry-making had already started, although it was still quite early in the morning. There were many Vincentians on hand who had come over the day before and had a head start.

The boats would race by class in groups of three to five

depending on how many were entered. The two whaleboats would be the last.

When there seemed to be no space left on the beach to stand and the crowd showed increasing restlessness, the Prime Minister made his appearance. He stood at the edge of the Frangipani's terrace with a bull horn in hand. Son Mitchell looked like anyone else from his dress. He wore an open-neck sport shirt and somewhat baggy trousers. He was quite tall, better than six feet. His features were well defined: thin face, high cheek bones, brown eyes, tan complexion, reminders that his grandmother was an Ollivierre, a French family that had settled on Bequia in the early 1800s.

"And now we come to the point that we have all been waiting for," Son shouted into his bull horn.

The applause and shouting and whistling began.

"Our very own boats, our fishing boats, made here on Bequia and sailed by Bequians!" Son had to shout into the bull horn for his voice to be heard over the din. He waited for the noise to diminish.

"I see that the first group in the 16 foot class is now ready. Is that correct?"

The crowd shouted approval.

"I will fire this pistol. That is the signal."

He waited a moment, held the pistol high in the air and fired. The two-man crews shoved their boats into the sea and climbed quickly aboard. The mainsail and jib were already up. The rudder was dropped into place and the mainsail was let out to catch the following trade wind. There were five boats in the first race. They were a colorful sight, hulls and sails in bright reds, blues, and yellows. They moved off quickly to the applause of the happy crowd.

When the first group was a quarter of a mile offshore, the next group prepared itself, and with a signal from the Prime Minister, they were on their way. There were 35 boats in all and it took several hours to get them on their way. The crowd remained but people began to mill about and visit with one another. Food was brought, or obtained from the nearby snackettes. Rum was in plentiful supply. Children became bored and moved down the beach to set up their cricket wickets. England has made at least two major contributions to the Caribbean islands: a parliamentary form of government and cricket.

The time had come for the whaleboat races. The Dart and Why Ask? were being prepared. Unlike the fishing boats, the whaleboats were facing the shore with their bows on the beach. Stone ballast was neatly piled in front of the boats. Their masts and furled sails lay on the open decks. The oars were next to the oar locks, ready to be dipped into the sea. It had always amazed me how a boat 26 feet in length, powered by the wind, could successfully chase, catch, and defeat a whale twice its length and weighing in the neighborhood of twenty-five tons.

"And now the last two whale boats in the whole Caribbean," Son bellowed and the crowd responded instantly with cheers, shouts, and applause. He paused a moment to allow the crowd to enjoy its response. Then he raised the starter pistol in the air and pulled the trigger.

The six-man crew of each of the whalers reacted quickly. Each crew formed a line, like a fire brigade, and quickly passed stone ballast to the last member, who carefully loaded the ballast on board. Four of the crew then jumped on board as the remaining two shoved the boat into the sea and climbed on board. Four oars were in the water in a flash and the fifth steered. The boats were quickly turned about to face the sea and now the rowing began. Why Ask? got off to a better start and kept its advantage. When the boats were several hundred yards out, far enough to catch the wind, the oars were brought in, the masts were stepped, and the sails unfurled and hoisted. The boats took off with great speed, better than ten knots, on their race to Friendship Bay and back. People stayed put until the boats disappeared around the bend.

The crowd now split up. Some remained to picnic on the beach. Others started the trek along the beach, over the hill at Belmont, to Princess Margaret Beach and beyond that to Lower Bay Beach. The dollar buses did a land-office business, taking people to Friendship Bay and Paget Farms, where they could see boats complete the first half of the race. By far the most popular spot was the Reefs at Lower Bay. There was a band playing there and Bequians and Vincentians danced and people were three deep at the bar. A main attraction of the Reefs is its location right on the beach. Here everything is available to you: a beautiful beach, a friendly bar, good and inexpensive food, and great atmosphere. It is very West Indian in its decor. Tables ring the concrete floor used for dances and table tennis. The walls are decorated with some old, weathered posters showing English scenes including the royal family in the royal garden, and flags of Great Britain and the U.S.A. (No French flags allowed). Vincentian, English, and American coins had been glued to the counter of the bar and some had been pried loose leaving spaces in the arrangement. Hanging over the bar are examples of local fish, nets and buoys.

Bequians can be noisy when they are having a good time and today they were having a good time. The crowd swelled and soon there was no space left at the bar or on the dance floor and very little on the beach. People had brought baskets of food and rum and were picnicking. Kids ran up and down the beach and another game of cricket had started. Families sat in groups in the shallow water, letting the gentle current cool their bodies. Competing with the steel band inside the Reefs were guitarists outside who sang calypso songs and attracted their own crowds.

I saw many familiar faces here. Sandy Meisner and Jimmy Carville had a table next to the dance floor. Violet Wallach was busy moving around, visiting with friends, and exchanging the latest information. Judy Simmons, who is the daughter of Father Ron Armstrong and June Armstrong, was on the beach with her husband, Mac, and their two children. Nobleman was at the bar drinking beer with friends. Dawn Simmons, one of the owners of the Reefs, was busy at the bar making drinks.

As sailboats came into view on the last leg back to the Frangipani, cheers went up and a new round of drinks was poured. Only a few returned to the Frangipani to watch the finish of the races. Most stayed put and partied that after-noon and through the night. Most Bequians went home finally, while many Vincentians, without lodging, slept the night on the beach.

The next morning was Easter and the beaches, inns, and

streets were very quiet. Women and children were all dressed up for church and the men, who had managed to survive the partying, came dressed in dark suits. They came from all over to attend services at the island's many churches. There was much singing in the churches. Many who could not get in stood outside listening to the singing and the services. It was a quiet, solemn, beautiful morning. The sun was bright and becoming warm. The birds twittered and for a change the dogs and chickens were quiet.

The Regatta began anew in the afternoon. All of the races had been completed, so all that was left was the awarding of prizes. The crowds began to gather right after lunch and by 3 p.m. the terrace of the Frangipani and the beach were as crowded as the day before. Son had several guests with him, including Herbert Blaze, Prime Minister of Grenada, and members of Parliament from Canada, and he was busy showing them around. As the day before, Son was casually dressed. His guests, however, chose to be more formal, particularly the ladies, who wouldn't have been more dressed if they were attending the races at Ascot. The Prime Minister now had a microphone available to him. Promptly at 3 p.m. he collected the crowd's attention.

"I would say this has been the best Regatta to date," he announced.

The crowd agreed with cheers and clapping. The winds, now increasing, played with his hair. He tried to brush it back with his hand.

"What's next on the agenda?" he teased.

"Bequia boats!" came the rejoinder, and the crowd became excited.

"Right!" he said. "Are you ready for the results?"

Everyone knew the results but that didn't matter. They wanted Son to tell them.

"In class one, the winner was Big Five, the runner up Bequia Sweet, and Pumpkin placed third!" The audience approved loudly. Not only were the winners popular boats, but Pumpkin was the Prince Minister's own boat and this was its debut.

Pumpkin was a sixteen foot fishing boat painted the color of a pumpkin. It had been constructed on the beach near the Frangipani.

There was little doubt concerning Son's popularity. For many years he had fought for the interests of Bequians as a member of St. Vincent's Parliament and only three years ago he and his party had won in a landslide victory and he was elected Prime Minister of St. Vincent and the Grenadines. His first step as Prime Minister was to abolish the ban on powdered and condensed milk which the previous administration had imposed in an effort to develop a local dairy industry. Son was a Bequian and the people loved him.

When he was elected Prime Minister, he promised Bequians two things: he would improve the roads and he would get an airport built on Bequia. Progress toward achieving these targets has not been as fast as Son had expected. He explains that he inherited many problems from the previous administration that must be answered before he can proceed with the roads and airport. People who know Son are positive that he will deliver on his promises. Son has a charisma about him that induces intense loyalty among his supporters, of whom there are many. He has much going for him. He is young, attractive, articulate and well educated. He graduated with honors from the London School of Economics, where, incidentally, he met Pat, his wife. They make a good team. Son splashes ideas around with a broad brush, Pat with a fine brush that is good for details. It seems to me that they are in the right place at the right time. Son has attracted considerable attention in the States and Europe, as well as the Caribbean. He has spoken frequently and articulately of the need for a confederation of Caribbean countries into a mini-state as the best and possibly the only solution to the problems and needs of the Caribbean. He is a man on the move and Bequia has made that possible.

Son announced the winners in all eight classes. Some of the winners were particularly popular. Donovan Ollivierre won easily in his class with his 21 foot Country Girl, and Pikie, a local taxi driver, won for the first time with his Lullu D in the 18 foot class.

Now Son came to the results of the whaleboat race.

"It makes me sad to realize," he said to the quieting crowd, "that we have just two whaleboats left on Bequia. At one time there were many and I can remember my father telling me how big an industry whaling once was. But we are fortunate that we still have two, for they are the only whaling vessels left in the whole Caribbean!"

Now the crowd cheered, almost on cue.

"The winner," he said, pausing a moment, "is Why Ask?"

The ovation was deafening. It was as though Why Ask?, which had been the favorite since it was captained by Athneal Ollivierre, had accomplished a miracle. Athneal was in the crowd but he resisted attempts to bring him up to the micro-phone. Like many seamen, his boldness is confined to the sea.

By this time Vincentians were back on the three large freighters that had brought them to Bequia on Thursday. One of the freighters had a steel band aboard which had no intention of letting up. The partying continued and the music and singing could be heard for a long time until the boats rounded the point and left the harbor.

The program had come to an end and people dispersed slowly, not quite ready to let go of what had been a glorious event. Son Mitchell stayed a while with his guests and then they left for the dining room.

It had been a grand weekend. I could not remember anything quite like it. Even the political rally a few years back, when Son was running for election, could not compare with it. Bequians are a kind of lay-back people, but they like a good time and that Easter weekend they certainly had it.

JIMMY CARVILLE

It was a beautiful morning to be making the crossing from Bequia to St. Vincent. The sun was already well up in the sky at seven in the morning. The air was so fresh that you wanted to package it and bring it home to the States. The sea can get very nasty in the 10 mile stretch when the trade winds blow in one direction and the tides move the other way. Today, it was as gentle as it ever gets.

The Friendship Rose, a schooner of about 115 feet in length, had all of its sails up to catch the wind. Between its engine and the wind, the boat could make the crossing in about an hour and a half, reaching St. Vincent at about eight, in time to have breakfast at the Heron before starting on the day's errands. The Rose's accommodations included two benches on the deck, one to port and the other to starboard, in addition to those in the cabin. The benches provided seating for about half the passengers. The rest sat on the cover over the hold, on top of the cabin, on crates, anywhere there was room. The Rose is the best buy in the Caribbean. For 5 E.C., about $2 U.S., you can make the 10 mile trip to St. Vincent. It is really an adventure because you may be sharing the deck with a bull secured to the bow, cases of Pepsi, a honeymoon couple still in their wedding clothes, an automobile strapped to the center deck, boxes of fresh bread for the Bequia stores, lumber, and plants from the Botanical Gardens. The return is at 12:30 noon, so you must move quickly if you have any amount of shopping to do.

I looked across to the lee side of the boat and saw Jimmy Carville and one of his students. They were both dozing, she with her head in his lap. I guessed that she had been feeling uneasy and that Jimmy had comforted her and in the process both had fallen asleep. It was a pleasing vignette.

Jimmy was going over to St. Vincent with his troupe from the Anglican High School to participate in an inter-island choral competition. This was the first time that Bequia children had entered the competition. Jimmy had only recently started the music class at the high school and wasn't very optimistic about their chances. "It's important that they try," he had said to me earlier, "Even if they fail, they will have had the experience."

Jimmy had been on the island only a few years. Bill Brown, who was the first principal of the high school, had invited Jimmy to teach music at the school, which he accepted. I remember Jimmy telling me about the experience. "I started with theory," Jimmy said. "Every kid had to learn the scales, notes and rhythms. I must say that Father Adams had a sense of the importance of the arts in education. He supported me every step of the way and I had problems in the beginning."

Jimmy had begun to make his mark on Bequia. He was outgoing, gregarious and very serious in his efforts to teach music to the children. People instinctively liked him. He had a friendly face, round, dimpled, smiling, and a full, handsome mustache, which later grew into a beard. He had one flaw. His body was short and did not seem to belong to his face. Sandy Meisner once said to him, "You have a leading man's face on a character actor's body." Jimmy had been amused rather than annoyed by the description, which was typical of Jimmy.

Jimmy was well qualified for his role as a teacher of music. After stints with Juliard and the American Theatre Wing, he started singing professionally in 1955 in musicals and concerts. He worked with the Scola Cantorum, which was made up of professional singers, and with Bernstein and Stokowski and with Tyrone Guthrie in productions at Stratford in Canada and after that in the Pirates of Penzance and Pinafore at the Phoenix Theatre in New York.

As Jimmy had feared, his group of children did not do well in the choral competition in St. Vincent. When I saw him the following evening, he said, "They were literally laughed off the stage. By Vincentian standards, Bequians are hicks and speak funny."

But that was the first year of competition. Jimmy worked very hard with his students, and they responded, and when they returned to St. Vincent the next year, they won the competition hands down, to the amazement of all.

As their talents developed, Jimmy gave them more

complex assignments. "I got the chorus involved in the Nine Lessons, which follow the Bible," he told me later on. "I tied it in with Christmas, with each of the lessons leading up to Christmas. A student reads the lesson and the chorus responds with two carols that are related to the lesson. We would start with the youngest student, then on to the older students, and then the last lesson was read by Son Mitchell. After that I got the idea that the Christmas section of the Messiah is based on the Nine Lessons and the songs are perfect to sing in each of the lessons, so what you wound up getting, in addition to the Nine Lessons, was the Christmas section of the Messiah. We did that on Christmas and after two years of that we started on the Easter section of the Messiah and I took that down to Paget Farm."

Jimmy's involvement with Gilbert & Sullivan in New York was only the beginning of his career. After that he was invited to join the National Chorus, a new organization being formed. It was to be a large pool of singers from which theatres throughout the country could select singers for their productions.

"They selected two singers from each state," Jimmy explained. "Edmund McCarthy of the Met did the selecting and I was picked for New York."

Jimmy and I were sitting on the terrace of the Sunny Caribee, waiting for Sandy. The Sunny Caribee was an old plantation house that had been restored. It was one of the most attractive places on the island.

"The Chorus had been formed by the National Brewers Association as part of an effort to raise the image of beer drinking," Jimmy said. "They were concerned with the image that beer was the drink of last resort. You know 'I'm sorry but all I have left in the house is beer.' In our first year we toured all of the towns where breweries were located. Unfortunately, the audiences misunderstood completely. They came prepared to see chorus girls, not choral singers. Well, the Chorus was disbanded and I went back to musicals. I hooked up with the Scola group again and sang opening night at Lincoln Center."

"When did you meet Sandy?" I asked

"Around 1959," Jimmy said. "I was working on Mozart's Abduction from the Seraglio and the pianist, who was working with me, told me about the American Musical Theatre Academy, a new study and repertory group. When I went there I told them that I didn't have the money to enroll and they said they thought I could get a scholarship, but first I would have to be interviewed by the head of their drama department, who was Sanford Meisner. I got the scholarship and enrolled, but the group went bust in its second year for lack of funds. That was in 1964. Sandy said he was going back to the Neighborhood Playhouse and he took 13 students with him including me. John Voigt was in the group. A little later Sandy sent me up to Harlem to head up the drama department for the School of the Arts in Harlem. We took several teachers from the Playhouse with us. I ran the drama department from 1966 to 1968. If you remember, Harlem started to burn in 1967. It became dangerous and I quit. I was getting tired of New York anyhow and Sandy was thinking of retiring."

Sandy arrived and joined us. Sandy looked well, robust. He had been swimming. He was still in his trunks with a towel wrapped around him. Although Jimmy was better known on the island, he was content to take a back seat to Sandy, who, afterall, was the star, the best teacher since Stanislavsky. Sandy called the waiter over and ordered drinks.

"Jimmy was telling me how you two met," I said.

"That's when you said to me that I had a leading man's face and a character actor's body," Jimmy said.

"I was right," Sandy replied.

"I remember his advice. He said to me, 'You are getting too old to be a chorus boy any longer. It's high time you're done with that. If they don't give you a decent role, get out. You don't have to take it. You can make money in other ways. Where do you think I would have gotten without teaching, a little Jew boy from Brooklyn?'"

Sandy smiled. "I'd still be in Brooklyn," he said.

"Sandy was thinking of retirement. One day he asked me if I would help him if he found land or a house in the Caribbean. I was fed up and said sure. So we started our search."

"We looked everywhere," Sandy said. "St. Thomas, St. John, St. Martin, Roatan."

"We got a concession for a laundramat in St. Martin and we were going to import Italian washing machines because they were part of the Common Market. Suddenly we discovered they had no water but were going to put in a desalinization plant," Jimmy said.

"I told him it would take years to do that," Sandy said.

"Next we went to the Bay Islands off Honduras, to Roatan," Jimmy said.

"We bought land, a banana plantation with a beautiful

beach," Sandy said. "And then I came down and went for a walk on the beach and was bitten alive by mosquitos."

"Why wasn't I bitten?" Jimmy said. "I was so busy planning the house that I never had a chance to go for a walk on the beach."

Ultimately they found Bequia.

"I circled December 17, 1968 on my calendar," Jimmy said. "That was the day when we found Ross Lully and told him we wanted to buy land."

"He said to me that we had to have nuggets of gold to be able to buy land on Bequia," Sandy said. "I told him we had nuggets of gold. He offered us seven acres for $150,000. I told him we didn't need seven acres."

"Vernon Wallace was there and he was Lully's drinking partner," Jimmy said. "He got the biggest kick out of someone standing up to Lully. In typical West Indian fashion, he fell off his chair laughing. He turned to Sandy and said, 'I'll show you land and you won't need nuggets of gold.' "

"Wallace drove us to La Pomp," Sandy said, "I said 'There!' and pointed to the side of a hill overlooking Friendship Bay."

"I didn't agree," Jimmy said. "I wanted to be on the beach. Sandy prevailed when he told me to look around and see where local people built their homes."

"Well, we bought the land and built the house and Jimmy got involved teaching the children music," Sandy said.

"One of our early projects was a musical program for the opening of the high school," Jimmy said. "It was a big event. The Archbishop came from Guyana and the Bishop from Barbados and many members of the clergy from St. Vincent. The place was swarming with politicians from St. Vincent. We worked up a program of six songs. We started with Bach, then we did some Foster, next some African numbers. We ended with the Desirade. A girl who was a first year student was picked to speak the Desirade. Her name was Elvie. The program was broadcast on St. Vincent radio. It was the first time that anything was broadcast from Bequia. Every woman on Bequia was glued to a radio set. Afterwards they talked a lot about Elvie. 'She was so strong, so clear!' they said. There's an interesting ending to the story. Elvie today is a graduate of the University of Toronto, with a Masters in media.''

"I wasn't here for that event," I said. "But I came to the dance at Industry to raise money to complete the school. That's when Sidney McIntosh lost his Moke and his teeth.''

"I remember that," Jimmy said and laughed.

"He found his teeth," I said. "He found them under his Moke in the harbor. A dog was chewing on them.''

"I told you about the Messiah," Jimmy said. "We built up from that to Mozart's Requiem. That required an orchestra, so we rehearsed on St. Vincent, with the police department band. We rehearsed from Christmas to June. The performance was to commemorate the 100th anniversary of the Anglican Diocese. Our first performance was on Bequia, then we took it to St. Vincent, and finally to Grenada. The next big event was the Messiah in celebration of St. Vincent's Independence. The beauty of the things we did was that people were getting culture without even knowing it. We had just finished doing Jesus Christ, Superstar. That was in 1978.''

"It was a great period of my life," Jimmy said. "Bequia gave me something I never had. The feeling of real accomplishment. Of being wanted and needed. I didn't realize then the disappointments that lay ahead."

"What happened?" I asked.

"He ran out of steam," Sandy said.

The emphasis on 'he' reminded me that Sandy had never been as involved as Jimmy. Jimmy remained on the island for years at a time. Sandy made frequent trips to New York to teach at the Neighborhood Playhouse.

"After Superstar we got involved in two projects, the Messiah to commemorate St. Vincent's Independence and Porgy and Bess," Jimmy said. "A group from New York heard our performance of Superstar and promised to send down orchestrations for Porgy and Bess. I made several trips to New York to get the material and finally realized they were a lot of wind. I was terribly disappointed. Porgy and Bess would have been a natural."

"The next disaster was the Messiah," Sandy said.

"We started rehearsals for the Messiah on St. Vincent but only two people showed up. This was a great letdown coming after the Porgy and Bess disappointment. Remember what I said to you, Sandy?"

"You were angry," Sandy said.

"I said, 'We don't need this. If they can't get to a rehearsal and we can get all the way over from Bequia at five in the morning, baloney. It's not worth the trouble. They don't appreciate what we are doing. And why are we forcing it down their throats?'"

"He was a glutton for punishment," Sandy said.

"We had still another fiasco," Jimmy said. "We were asked to put on Superstar on St. Vincent to help raise money for the hospital. People who were supposed to help with the production just didn't show up. The afternoon of the performance I was told by the Minister of Home Affairs that Sandy owed them six thousand dollars. 'What for? We are doing this to raise money for sheets and pillow cases for the hospital!' I was told that the money was for the wires and wood for the stage and for incidentals. I blew up. I said, 'We are not paying a dime, take it all back, and we are not doing the show.' A representative of the hospital interceded and persuaded the Minister to reverse his position. So we went ahead with the show. In the middle of the performance, microphones were being removed by a group that needed them for a dance that evening. It was like something out of the Marx Brothers. They took the mikes, all but three, while the show was going on. The kids were real troupers. They went on with the show. They passed the three mikes around and we finally finished the performance."

"That's when I quit," Jimmy said. "I had it up to here."

Sandy was getting impatient. He was obviously uncomfortable in his wet suit and wanted to return home. Jimmy was quite comfortable but acquiesced.

"He's getting itchy," Jimmy said. "We'll pick this up another time."

But it wasn't until many years later that I heard the rest of the story. I had been attending Sandy's drama workshop and moved to the terrace with the students when it was time for lunch. Jimmy was very much involved in the workshops. He helped in selecting the applicants who would be invited, arranged for their transportation to Bequia, booked accommodations for them and worked in the kitchen with Winnie preparing the lunches. There was no way that Sandy could have had his workshop without the help of Jimmy. After lunch Sandy returned to his studio with his students and I remained behind with Jimmy.

"When did Sandy get cancer?" I asked.

"In 1978," Jimmy said. "That was a bad year. After our troubles with the Minister of Home Affairs, we decided we needed a rest and went to Greece on vacation. That was the end of almost ten years of work on the island. After our vacation, we returned to New York with the idea of doing commercials and helping Pollack with his work videotaping Sandy's drama classes in New York. At about this time the Neighborhood Playhouse was left without a director or secretary. Both died within days of one another. Sandy took over the job of running the Playhouse until he got hit by a truck. That was in 1983. We didn't get back to Bequia until the following year. We realized then we could not just sit and look at four walls. It was then that we decided to start the drama workshop on Bequia."

"Bequia has meant more to you than Sandy," I said.

"I was more involved, and when things came apart, I was hurt more. In spite of Sandy's ailments, he still had the Neighborhood Playhouse."

"Is the workshop really working?"

"This is our third year. Yes, it is successful, very."

"I mean in filling a void in both your lives."

"It is more important to Sandy. He couldn't survive here without it. I am involved in putting it together, but I could

97

be doing other things as well. Well, maybe. I don't think I could go back to teaching music and putting on shows. That's over with.''

"You came here in search of paradise," I said.

"We had it once. Paradise is elusive. It can slip through your fingers without you even knowing it.'' He paused, looked me straight in the eye, and smiled. "It's not really lost. Just mislaid.''

NOBLEMAN

I was standing on the Frangipani pier watching the fishing boats being readied for the second day of the Easter Regatta. Nobleman was passing from boat to boat checking them out and talking with the skippers. I caught up with him and we sat down on the beach, waiting for the races to start.

Nobleman was like other Bequians in some ways and different in others. He shared with his peers a strong love for the island. He showed that by coming back to Bequia after 18 years abroad. But his years away gave him a perspective that was unusual on the island. He was quite articulate, particularly when politics entered the conversation. He was one of the best cabbies on the island but he didn't scramble for business like the other drivers. He was quite content to park his blue cab across the street from Tannis' store in the harbor and wait for his steady customers to seek him out. When he wasn't driving, he was fixing cars and he was good at that. In all the years that I had known Nobleman, his cab never broke down, and I didn't know of another cabbie who could make that claim. Like most Bequians, he had no interest in working on the land. That was for Vincentians. If he didn't have a fare or a car to fix, he would just as soon sit at Tannis' bar, have a beer, and talk. After all, he was at heart a seafarer.

Nobleman was short and well built. He had a round face and eyes that sparkled when he got on to a subject that interested him. His beard was neatly trimmed, with a touch of gray to match his sideburns. He claimed that gray signified virility, which was followed by a deep laugh and the exclamation 'crazy'. He liked to use that word to highlight a statement that was unbelievable, or far out.

"Who's going to win?" I asked.

"Country Girl," Nobleman replied.

"That's Donovan's boat."

"I don know if she is his," Nobleman said. "But he is sailing she."

"Why aren't you in the race?"

"Too busy."

"Taxiing?"

"Dat and fixin cars."

"I understand you are a good mechanic."

"Ah, yes. I take dat up in England. I went to college, automotive mechanic college. When I reach England, all I know is the sea. Now, I had a skill, certified, and I brought it home."

"I'm told you've been to Africa."

"Before goin to England, I shipped wid freighters. On

one voyage, I sailed from St. Vincent to Barbados, then to Caracas, then to Argentina. Here we loaded down with soy beans for Russia. We sailed trough the Black Sea to Russia, the same spot where the Germans invaded Russia. Ship got orders to go to Liberia in Africa. We take coal dere to Europe. The whole trip took four months.''

"Let's find some place more comfortable," I said, and we got up and went to the Frangipani and plunked ourselves down in big wooden chairs on the terrace, facing the sea.

Donovan's boat, Country Girl, was in the first heat, along with four other twenty-one foot fishing boats. Their sterns were on the beach and their bows to sea. The Prime Minister was standing on the edge of the beach with a starter pistol in the air. He counted one, two, and a shot exploded and the boats were off. Country Girl took the lead and we followed them until they disappeared from sight.

"When did you start sailing?" I asked.

"I was seventeen. I crewed on boats dat sailed around the Caribbean. When I came to Trinidad I saw a poster when I pass trough customs and it says come to England where every man's home is his castle. They says dat England's the place. You goes dere and makes some fast bucks and you come home and do your ting. No problem getting there. In dose days we were British subjects and we could go anywhere in the Commonwealth.''

"I heard you play the trumpet at the jump-up at Industry a few weeks ago," I said. "You were pretty good. Did you learn to play in England?''

"Self-taught," he said. "When I was a young man, I was inventive, with music. I remember starting work on a schooner as messman. Fus place I went was Trinidad. Dere's a store we call the Salvatores Cat. I looked through the window and I saw a trumpet for $120. And I was working for five dollars a month. How could I get this trumpet? I made another trip to Trinidad and den I jumped ship and went to work for nine months and I bought my trumpet and came home as a stowaway. When I bought the trumpet I got a self-help book and I learned to play. I learned the first C and the first G and the book did the rest. The first ting I played was Santa Lucia. Later, when I was in England I heard Santa Lucia played for the first time and it sounded exactly like me.''

"When did you go to England?''

"I was twenty-one. Dat was in 1957. I got a job in a steel mill in Leeds. I worked in the foundry and cast parts for gear boxes, frames, all automotive. I also drove a crane and became machine operator. I did profile burnin and drillin. Done a bit of everytin. Reached to semi-skill but that was not good enough, so I went to college and became auto mechanic.''

"What happened to your music?''

"I also did dat. I had a band and we played for working man's clubs, midnight clubs and dat sorta ting. We played all kinds of music. We wus a favorite with the army at Harrigate. We played for the army one Saturday night every month. We played jazz, rock and roll, calypso, everytin. One day I joined the territorial army and wus accepted as a bandsman. The food wus good but I didn't like der ways much. I had a girl friend back home and I wrote for her to come over and I sent her a ticket. Her name was Elsa and we got married. I have a daughter, Susan, who was born on Bequia, and she works now in Trinidad as a secretary with a printer. After I got out of the army, we decided to come home. England wus okay, but too cold. Besides, now I have a trade, auto mechanic, which I cud use back home.''

It was very pleasant sitting on the Frangipani terrace, looking out to sea, with the trade winds to our back, and the overhead coconut fronds shielding us from the late morning sun. The races were still going on but I had lost track. I fetched beers for Nobleman and for myself.

"I guess things haven't changed much since you were a kid," I said.

"Ah, yes. Dey change like day to night. One time we had it all. We wus British subjects. We cud sail anywhere, Honduras, Guatamala, Venezuela and we didn't need passports. Immigration jes check der list and we go away and nobody aks questions. Yahs, we had it all. But dey so damn greedy. Say Englishman not giving enough, so dey fool the people dey will get more and dey aks for independence. Each island, one by one, get independent. Can't beg England alone now, they want to beg the world. All goin bankrupt. Jamaica, Trinidad, Guyana. We had it all and we trowed it away. Crazy, man, crazy. We is better off here and tank God for dat.''

"Seems to me you've done pretty well," I said.

"Anything I set my mind to I get. You don't sit down and say please can I have dis or dat. You works. I am satisfied with small tings. I know what is possible and what is not. I learned dat when I was young. Dat doesn't mean I get shoved around. No. suh.''

103

"We not so free as we used to be. You run into difficult people wherever you go. You see dey imitating der bosses and der bosses imitating der ones way up. Dey make it difficult so you need a passport and a visa to go anywhere. Crazy aint it? Many of the islands is in trouble. The politician bankrupts the country and the little man suffers. He promises you dis and he promises you dat. Der should be a way to take him down where he doesn't do his promises. In Lancashire, when I wus in England, a district pulled down its representative. We called on the Prime Minister to invoke his ting. We said he no longer represents us. We had an election and we got him out."

The beach and the terrace were filling up with happy, noisy people. Most everyone you knew passed by one time or another. I saw Father Armstrong and his wife, June, in the distance and waved to them.

"I've never seen so many people in one place," I said.

"If any more people come on the island, it's goin to sink," Nobleman said. "Crazy."

Kids farther down the beach were playing cricket. Family groups were sitting in the water, cooling off. Blankets were spread on the sand and people were having picnics, laughing, shouting, having a good time.

"First ting we got to learn is how to keep our house in order. Good housekeeping, yes suh. The British wus teaching us dat. We forgot the lesson and now too many governments just spend and spend and spend. Dey is living on borrowed time. Now and den governments change, but the new government finds the treasury empty. Das the kind of problem Son walked into and is going to take time to straighten out."

"Amen," I said.

Nobleman looked at me and his serious look broke into a smile. "Crazy," he said.

"Nobleman, you've got a great name," I said. "Where did you get it?"

"Ders not much of a story to tell," he said. "My title is Philips and my given name Newman. My mother changed Newman to Novaman, which means the same but she likes it better. Novaman sounded like Nobleman, so my name became Nobleman. I like the name. It has a nice sound. Crazy."

I never noticed that Nobleman had any difficulty with the name. It seemed to fit and he wore it well. I also liked the sound and the image it conveyed.

"Do you ever wish you were back in England?" I asked.

"Not really. You can make money der, but ders more to livin than money. Nobody hassles you here. We got problems but I'd rather deal wid ours than yours. I know what I can do here and I am happy. Dis is my island, you see. I belongs here. You are welcome here, too, but der are places out der where I don't see the welcome mat because der aint' any."

BULU

I first met Bulu at a dinner party given by Jimmy Carville and Sandy Meisner in the home they shared at La Pomp. That was about fifteen years ago. It was a pleasant evening, I remember, with a light breeze blowing from the east. Dusk was short and night came quickly, which is normal in the tropics. Earlier we had watched for the green flash from the sun setting on the sea, a spectacular scene when it happens. I have never heard a plausible explanation for the green flash. In any event, it did not occur this evening.

I was having cocktails with other guests on the terrace, when Bulu appeared in the doorway of the living room. He was a strange sight, barefooted, dressed in snug black trousers and a bright red jacket like the kind you used to see on "Johnny" in Philip Morris commercials. He was just a boy, a black boy, about fourteen. He hesitated for a moment and then came over to where I was sitting. He looked uneasy and focused his eyes on the floor and then announced in a deep halting monotone, "Dinner . . .is. . .now. . .being. . . served." He then went around the terrace to the other guests, making the same announcement in the dreary voice belonging to the deaf. When he finished his announcements, he departed, and I saw him a few minutes later in the dining room, helping Winnie, the cook, serve dinner.

Bulu's appearance took me by surprise. I had heard about this kid, who people said was wild, and I had seen him several times, usually in remote parts of the island, but never closeup. It seemed to me that he was always running away from something, or somebody. I asked Jimmy about this at dinner.

"You would too, if you were confined in a pen, like an animal, by a crazy aunt," Jimmy said.

There was a note of mild indignation in Jimmy's voice. It wasn't that he was really indignant. It was his way of expressing himself. He tended to be dramatic, which was not surprising, considering his theatrical background.

An elegant dinner was served. Winnie was the cook officially. But Jimmy was more than a little involved. He delighted in preparing unusual dishes.

"People say his aunt is a witch," I said.

"She is plain crazy," Jimmy said. "Ask anybody in Paget. They'll tell you his aunt is funny in the head."

"What do they say about Bulu?"

"Same thing. But he isn't. He's deaf but as sane as anybody."

"He seems frightened," I said.

"He's scared of just about everyone. We're his only friends, I think, Winnie, Sandy and I. And it took some time

107

before he trusted us. He was a terrible sight when I found him on a pile of rags in my garage.''

"I'm surprised he didn't run.''

"He didn't have the strength. He was really beat. It was Winnie who was able to persuade him to stay. She's related to him somehow. Everyone in Paget is related in some way.''

"What's his chances?''

"Pretty good. I've been working with him to read lips and I got him a hearing aid. Announcing dinner tonight was no small accomplishment. It took a lot of rehearsing.''

Bulu was helping Winnie serve dinner. He was doing quite well, I thought. He spilled a little wine while filling my glass. He seemed a little nervous. I looked the other way, as though I had not noticed the accident.

"He's a big help," Jimmy said. "He's really more than that. He's like a member of the family.''

I could not think of anyone I knew who was like Jimmy. Who else would have taken a black boy, presumably wild, into his home and treated him like family? There were times when I thought Jimmy was too good to be true. He was always doing things for people. I thought back to the time when he came to the island several years ago. One of the first things that he did was to persuade Father Adams to let him work with the children at the Anglican Church and in practically no time he had them singing like birds. His satisfaction, he said at the time, was the reward of creating something from nothing, like a gardener's when he sees blossoms burst forth from what was once a bare piece of ground.

I looked across the table at Jimmy, who was now engaged in a conversation with a local person, a black lady, who ran one of the shops in Port Elizabeth. She was obviously pleased to receive his attention. Jimmy, I thought, could charm anyone. He made a striking appearance, with his new full beard, wavy gray hair, and eyes that could be deep and serious one moment and mischievous the next.

I did not see Jimmy or Bulu again for almost a year. When I returned to Bequia the following winter, I learned that the choral group Jimmy had organized at the Anglican Church had won first prize in the annual inter-island competition in St. Vincent. I also learned that Jimmy was embarked on his most ambitious undertaking to date, the staging of Jesus Christ, Superstar, with a cast of local children.

The big night was now at hand. When I arrived at the open arena in the coconut grove where the musical was being performed, it was already in progress. My eyes drifted over the performers, most of whom I recognized. I sat upright with a start. I could not believe my eyes. There was Bulu playing the bass drum!

The show was a tremendous success. The local people were visibly moved by the play. They shouted and they clapped and they giggled, all of which meant they approved. The costuming was improvised and the acting was a little unpolished, but the singing was first rate and Bulu was sensational.

"I would never have believed it possible," I told Jimmy afterwards, when we ended up at the familiar kidney-shaped table at the bar in the Frangipani. "I mean Bulu."

"I knew he could do it," Jimmy responded.

"I still don't understand how he was able to handle the drums," I said.

"He can feel the vibration of the music, and did you watch him? He followed my baton like a hawk."

It had been a very exciting experience. I was amazed that a group of amateurs on a remote tropical island could turn in such a remarkable performance. There was a group of us now at the round table, mostly Americans and a few Europeans. Jimmy was the center of attention. I sat back and listened. Jimmy was at his best when he talked about the theatre, about which he knew a great deal.

Bulu had been standing in the shadows. He was watching and listening. He was too shy to move into the center of things. Jimmy spotted him and motioned him to come over. He pulled a chair over for Bulu.

"Bulu, you know everyone?"

Bulu nodded and sat down.

"These gentlemen say you did a super job."

Bulu beamed.

"I think you did, too. You know why? You worked your tail off!"

Bulu nodded and broke into a grin.

"You de boss!" he grunted. "You de boss!"

"Bulu has been with me now for about two years. When we first met he couldn't say a blessed word. Now listen to him!" Jimmy slapped Bulu on the knee. "Bulu, these people would like to know how you were able to play the drums."

"I feel it in my toes, and I watch you like you say."

Word got around to the neighboring islands of Jimmy's success with Jesus Christ, Superstar and he agreed to put on another performance, which was attended by a number of dignitaries, including the Governor-General and his wife,

110

and a flock of English people from nearby Mustique.

The following year I decided to spend Christmas on the island. I had never done that before. I understood it was very different. You had to squint very tightly, I was told, to make white beaches look like snow, and you had to have a fertile imagination to look at a norfolk pine and see a Christmas spruce. But there were many parties and God forbid that you would need a plumber, or a carpenter, or an electrician anytime between December 15 and January 15, when practically all work on the island ceased for the holidays.

I arrived on Bequia about a week before Christmas. I was sitting at a table at the Frangipani having an elevensee, a morning drink that precedes the sun-over-the-yardarm by sixty minutes. You don't have to sit there very long before you've met just about everyone on the island. There's constant traffic from Port Elizabeth to the many shops along the beach, and the Frangipani, conveniently located at mid-point, catches much of the traffic. Jimmy usually stopped in just before noon. Today, he was right on schedule.

He grabbed my hand and shook it vigorously.

"When did you arrive?"

"Yesterday afternoon on the Friendship Rose," I replied.

Jimmy looked about the same. He didn't seem any older, except that his hair was longer and his beard fuller. His complexion caught my attention. His skin was pink and unlined and almost boyish. It's odd, I thought, that I had not noticed that before.

"Tell me what's going on," I said.

"Well, we have had an election and the right people won. There's talk about a small airport and a group of people have

111

gotten together to start a whaling museum."

"I saw Bulu on the street yesterday when I arrived. He looked great and he stopped to say hello. He's lost a lot of his shyness."

"I've got a new project," Jimmy announced.

"Oh?"

"I'm going to bring Santa to Bequia," he said.

I looked incredulous and I could see he was amused.

"It's a pity that kids grow up on this island and never know Santa Claus. So I have decided to intervene. I'm going to bring Santa here."

"I can't keep up with you," I said.

He settled back in his chair and smiled. He looked like Santa, I thought, white curly hair, full beard, dimpled cheeks. I noticed that he had gotten a little paunchy. Good casting, I thought.

"I've gotten hold of a large rubber raft with a sail and a motor," he said. "We plan to leave early Christmas morning, sail around Moonhole, and come ashore at the dock in Port Elizabeth around ten. Winnie is making our costumes. She's made a Santa outfit out of cheesecloth and has dyed it red, and sewn on bands of cotton for trim. Bulu's outfit is fantastic. I found a white Nehru jacket and tight-fitting white pants like the kind Indians wear, and Winnie fancied up the outfit with a gold belt and gold buttons. Bulu looks terrific in it."

"I don't understand Bulu's role," I said.

"In the Dutch tradition, Santa has a helper, who is black, and is dressed in white and gold. He carries a scepter. Well, I've made him a staff and painted it gold. He's crazy about

112

his costume. He tries it on every evening and I have quite a time getting him to take it off before retiring."

"What about gifts?" I asked.

"We've got gifts. Your friend, Violet, brought down cartons of gifts. Others have contributed too. Everyone's cooperating. The Friendly Society is contributing a steel drum band to welcome us when we come ashore," he said.

"Sounds fantastic," I said. "I would like to take some pictures."

"Fine. Get to my house early Christmas morning," he said. "I'd like to come ashore in the harbor around eleven."

I was at his house before nine Christmas morning several days later. I started to take pictures at once. I shot pictures of Jimmy and Bulu getting dressed in their costumes, having breakfast, packing their bags of gifts, carrying them down to the beach, getting into the big rubber raft with an outboard engine, and departing for Port Elizabeth. It was a pleasantly warm morning. The sun was bright, the sky very blue, and the sea was relatively calm. There was a light breeze blowing, which was a pleasant surprise. Usually this time of year the trade winds are very strong and relentless. They call them the Christmas winds in the tropics.

I got into my Moke and drove to Port Elizabeth, which was only about ten minutes away by car, but almost an hour by boat. The word had spread that Santa was coming to Bequia and there was already a crowd of youngsters and adults waiting at the dock and along the beach and on the main road which paralleled the beach. The children chased back and forth along the beach. They were excited and noisy and more restless than usual.

The beautiful harbor was filled with sailboats from many parts of the world.

I think I was the first to spot the rubber raft come around the point. Violet Wallach was with me on the terrace of the Frangipani. We hurried over to the jetty. In a matter of moments you could hear a stirring among the crowd, and it became increasingly louder as more recognized the boat carrying Santa and his helper. Soon the air was a cacophony of shrieks, shouts, handclapping, whistles, just about every sound that would denote the combination of excitement and joy. When the raft pulled up alongside the dock, there were many hands to take the rope from the boat. At that moment the band started playing an island version of "Jingle Bells" on steel drums.

Jimmy and Bulu were helped out of the boat by so many well-wishers that for a moment it looked as though they would be shoved into the sea. A couple of policemen, dressed in white jackets and black trousers, with a bright red stripe down the side, came to the rescue, and just in time.

For a moment the shoving stopped and a hush came over the crowd, as it admired the spectacle of Santa and his helper standing there in their beautiful regalia. The silence was broken when Santa shouted out in a loud voice, "Merry Christmas!"

By now the crowd numbered at least several hundred and they all responded at once, "Merry Christmas!" in a deafening roar.

The procession started up. The truck with the steel band headed the procession, then came Bulu with his golden staff, and finally Santa who pranced about and waved and blew kisses and shouted greetings to the hundreds more who lined the streets on the way to the elementary school a few blocks away. Violet and I joined the crowd and tried to keep up with Santa and his helper.

"Don he look grand!" a boy next to me said.

"Dats Mister Jimmy!" another shouted.

"Is you sure?"

"I wud know him anywhere. Dat's he all right!"

"I know dat right along," another said.

"How come you know dat?"

"Meester Jimmy has been on Bequia for many years and I know he is Santa. I been waiting all dis time for him to reveal hisself."

"Now look at that boy, Bulu! I never know him look like dat!"

"You tought he was a dummy, I bet. But I know better. He don't hear good, but he's smart. Look at he dere. Look at the big grin on his face and see de way he waves that yaller stick. Boy, he looks like he owns de world! I never tell you but he and me are good friends!"

The procession moved slowly and finally it reached the entrance to the elementary school, where the crowd behind and to each side converged on Santa and his helper. Fortunately, the police were there to maintain order. To the tune of "God Rest You Merry Gentlemen," played on Esso steel drums, children and their parents filed into the building and noisily proceeded to the auditorium where the rest of the presents that Santa and his helper couldn't carry had been brought earlier and stacked in neat piles around the Christmas tree. The tree was not exactly a specimen tree, but it looked as good as a norfolk pine could look and was the nearest thing to a spruce that you could find in the tropics. Santa sat in a big planter's chair, with the leg racks folded back out of the way, and Bulu stood at his side.

It was a small auditorium and jammed full with excited, noisy, happy children, and their equally excited, noisy and happy parents. Bulu's job was to pass the gifts to Santa who handed them out to the children and also to their parents, who weren't about to leave empty-handed. Santa knew practically all of them by name, so he had appropriate messages.

"Quashie," Jimmy said to the boy at the head of the line, "I understand that you are doing better at school this year. That's good. Here, I have a present for you."

The boy beamed, took his present and ran.

The giving of presents lasted into the afternoon and when it was over Santa and his helper were beat and so was Violet who stayed to the end. It was an unusual event and Bequia talked about it for a very long time.

The next time I saw Jimmy was the following summer in New York. I rang the bell to his apartment and was surprised when Bulu answered the door. He grinned, a big, happy grin.

"I didn't expect to see you!" I said.

"Wel-come!" he practically shouted.

Jimmy met me in the hallway.

"I thought you would be surprised," he said. "Bulu came back with me. I got him a temporary visa."

Bulu had grown a mustache and looked older and more sure of himself.

"How long have you been here?"

116

"About three months," Jimmy answered for him.

"How are you getting along?" I asked.

"I know the F train and the E train and the buses," Bulu answered proudly. "I get along fine."

He still spoke in a monotone, which was to be expected, but he was more fluent and he didn't hesitate between words as much as when I first met him.

"Tell Tom about the discos," Jimmy said.

Bulu beamed. "I go most every night." He saw my astonishment and beamed even more broadly. "I hear better and I feel the music better."

"Bulu has his favorite disco," Jimmy said. "He doesn't bother with queues. He moves right to the front of the line and they let him in. They like him. They gave him a job. He goes back in the morning to help clean up."

"I go to Hunter," Bulu announced. "Three times a week."

"Hunter has taken an interest in Bulu," Jimmy explained. "He's got better than average intelligence, they say, and they're trying to help him catch up."

"Do you miss home?" I asked.

"Mister Tom," he said. "Dis is my home."

I looked at Jimmy. He seemed quite pleased. I thought again of the flower that came from nowhere.

I saw Bulu again some years later at the dedication of the Sanford Meisner Theatre in New York. The audience was comprised of friends and famous people who had been students of Sandy. At the appropriate moment Sandy would be led down the center aisle to the stage. Bulu was selected for the honor of accompanying him. I remember Bulu leading

Sandy to the stage. He looked magnificent in the well-tailored gray suit that Rusty Ford had lent to him. The event was on television and photos appeared in many newspapers.

Probably not that night, but at some point in time, the thought must have crossed Bulu's mind that he owed his happy presence in New York to the magic of Bequia that enticed and then captured the hearts of Jimmy and Sandy.

THE ARMSTRONGS

Father Ron Armstrong does not fit the image that most people have of a clergyman. He wears his collar only when he has to and that is during the conduct of a service. He frequently rides around Bequia on a Honda motorbike. He is involved in many activities that are only remotely connected with his clerical duties. He looks more like a slightly aging athlete than a minister.

An Anglican minister, he came to Bequia with his wife, June, when he retired from the ministry in Toronto in 1980. Retirement is not an apt word to describe their status. They work harder and longer hours than anyone I have ever met. Fortunately, they enjoy their work and you get the impression from talking with them that they have always worked to the limit of their abilities.

The Armstrongs live in a modest home at La Pomp on the road to Paget Farm. They get around now with a car that was donated by a charity in Canada. Sometimes they use a two-passenger Honda motor bike. They make quite a picture, the Reverend Father and his wife scooting around Bequia on a motor bike.

Their accomplishments are well known on the island.

They helped start the School for the Deaf and run it.

They started and still direct a Workshop for the Handicapped.

They started the School for the Handicapped and run it.

They are responsible for bringing in tons of medical supplies and educational materials every year.

Their mission sponsors over 100 children and young adults at various schools on the island.

Twice a year they bring down work parties of about 20 Canadians to paint, make repairs, and teach.

They receive all kinds of gifts from Canadian people and businesses and they make sure they are put to optimum use.

Ron, June, and I were having croissants and coffee on the porch of Mac's Pizza, a charming and successful restaurant and bakery, which their daughter, Judy, started a few years ago.

"Sometimes the gifts we receive are a little off-beat but we take them anyway," Ron said and smiled. "I'll never forget the container-load of yellow toilet paper we received. As you know, toilet paper is a precious commodity in the tropics, so we had no problem putting it to good use. For a long time afterwards you could find bright yellow toilet paper in every public place on Bequia and some of the other islands — in clinics, schools, government offices. Everywhere."

In addition to their charitable work, Ron is full-time minister of the Anglican Church at Paget Farm and June is his aide.

They work well as a team. Ron, the seer in touch with the world beyond. June, the practical, business-like supporter and doer. Ron, fair-haired, well-built, young in appearance and spirit; June, outgoing, business-like, the typical dean of women at a New England college.

It is amazing that neither shows any signs of fatigue. They both seem to have reservoirs of inner strength that enable them to look composed, cheerful, and optimistic.

The vehicle for their activities is the Bequia Mission, which they started in 1980. The mission is funded by a group of about 400 Canadians who are friends and supporters of the Armstrongs.

The Armstrongs first became involved with Bequia in 1970. Their daughter, Mary, had worked with retarded children in Canada, and came to Bequia on a sabbatical and became interested in the children at the high school. She was concerned with their reading ability and ordered a remedial reading program from the States. It cost $1500, which she didn't have but was able to raise. The Armstrongs became interested in Bequia and formed the Friends of Bequia, a group of about 35, to help. Ten years later, when they retired, the Bequia Mission was incorporated to carry on the work of the Friends on an expanded scale.

"When we retired we cut ourselves off from our pension funds, insurance and income," Ron explained.

"And we disposed of all our material possessions," June added.

"It was really not as bad as it sounds," Ron said. "We had anticipated retirement long before, and we had saved enough to be able to make the move."

June explains the move this way. "We had given two-thirds of our lives working within the parameters of the church's hierarchy. We decided to give the remaining third in our own way, doing what we felt was important, unfettered by possessions and supervision."

When I talked with the Armstrongs about their experiences before coming to Bequia, it became apparent that the thirty five years of working within the ministry in Toronto had prepared them for the challenges they undertook in retirement, and may, indeed, have been designed to serve that purpose.

Ron's involvement with the church began when he was in the seventh grade. World War II had broken out. He was very disturbed by the war. "I thought I would try to bring peace into people's lives through the church," Ron said. "I took my training at Wycliff, which is part of the University of Toronto, and was ordained in 1953."

"We were married at the time," June said.

"At first the hierarchy was against our marrying before I completed my studies, but finally they consented."

Ron held a number of ministerial posts in the Toronto area. Ron and June are mavericks. They like to build and they like to eliminate red tape and bring about change and improvement. They built two churches and four parishes. One was the first to introduce guitar music in the service. They established a school for lay ministry and they took the lead in arguing for women serving in the sanctuary.

It was when he was associated with St. Elizabeth's Church in Etokicoke, Toronto, that he had a pentacostal experience.

"That was in 1960," he said. "The renewal movement within the Anglican Church began in that year. It started in the living room of our home, with a meeting of three nuns, a Polish layman who could hardly speak English, and myself. We all had had pentacostal experiences, speaking in tongues, languages that are unknown."

"Another name for it is the charismatic movement," said June.

"When you talk about the charismatic movement," Ron explained, "you are talking about the supernatural activity of God, the Holy Spirit, which manifests itself in many ways, such as speaking in tongues, healing, and gifts of knowledge. Athneal Ollivierre is a very charismatic personality. He has had many visions and has described them to me."

Ron describes his experience as suddenly coming alive in a new way within the Holy Spirit, a kind of re-birth. "Within two weeks of when this happened, we encountered eight young people in the parish who had had the same experience. I went to the Bishop and said something was happening. The Bishop said that it was important that there be apostolic supervision of the experiences and he approved of my establishing a teaching center. The Bishop said that he could not be identified with it, since it was strange, new, unknown. I was 35 at the time and happily accepted the challenge."

Ron organized meetings to which people who had similar experiences were invited to attend. Several hundred attended the Friday meetings and they went on for several years.

123

"When I left St. Elizabeth, I became involved with education," he said. "Community colleges were new in Ontario at the time and my job was to help develop a campus to serve as a proving ground for new ideas."

"We had worked pretty hard and needed a breather so we took a vacation and went to Bequia where our daughter, Mary, was working with the high school children," June said. "We quickly realized that Bequia would be our retirement place 10 years later."

"The Bequia Mission today has a budget of $100,000 and our charter describes three areas of activity: education, religion, and social service. We have a board of directors who are elected by members of the Mission."

"I understand that you were responsible for building a laboratory at the medical clinic," I said.

"That was our big thrust this year. We now have a lab and it is working fine. You know Eric Rogers? Well, he came down on one of our work parties three years ago. He has now retired from his medical practice and together with his wife, who is a nurse, devotes a large part of his time to the clinic."

"We brought down four tons of medical and educational supplies last year," June said. "I wouldn't be surprised if every bandage, crutch and wheelchair on the island is furnished by the Mission."

"We send down everything imaginable," Ron said, "school supplies, copying machines, typewriters, guitars, children's books, and all kinds of clothing."

Arrival of a shipment usually generates a lot of excitement on the island. The goods are often sighted long before

124

the Armstrongs know of their imminent arrival. Containers are spotted on the docks in St. Vincent and word quickly reaches Bequia that the Armstrong shipment is close at hand.

"We get all kinds of requests," June said. "A worker in the church calls: 'Father, the Lords blest me wid six kids, but no job. Ahs can use anytin.' Or: 'Mrs. Armstrong, find me a ball. Last time Prostis got two and none fer me.'"

One request is likely to remain indelibly impressed in June's memory. It was made by Lillian, one of the island's characters. Appearing in the doorway of the mortuary where the crates are unpacked, Lillian reached into the depths of her dress and pulled out a very ample breast.

"Anything for this size?" she said. "I surely need some real bad."

"I hastily agreed to look for a size 44 brassiere," June said. With that assurance, Lillian tucked her incredible breast back into her dress and left.

The shipping crates have many uses. They turn up all over the island as tables, storage boxes for vegetables, garbage bins, dog houses, chicken coops.

"We use the mortuary to unpack the crates," June said, "first because of its size, and second because nobody is likely to break into the mortuary where jumbies may be found."

"Everything can be running pretty smoothly," Ron said, "and all of a sudden we run into a language problem. That may sound strange, since English is their language. We were having a committee meeting and I remember saying 'Let's not be too hasty about this,' and I looked around and saw a strange look on all of their faces. Finally, one member of the committee explained that hasty meant bad tempered. To call a woman a hasty woman is to say that she is a shrew."

On another occasion June decided to step in and rid the school room of a slightly tipsy young man who was hindering the day's program.

"You must go," June said. "You have been interfering with the teacher."

"Interfering," he shieked. "What interfering? How you say I am interfering? That's a bad ting to say by me. I no believe you lie so bad. I never, never interfering.

"At the time I thought the young man was overreacting until one of the teachers told me that interfering was akin to rape."

"Our work here has its amusing side," June continued. "Bequians are lovely people and at times they are downright funny and thank God for that. They make the work worth while."

I asked how much help they had.

"We're very thin," Ron replied. "June and I do most of the work. Right now we are involved in a number of new projects. We're sending supplies to the other islands, Canouan, Union, Mayreau. Shortly we will be sending a work party to St. Vincent to paint, make repairs, and install a new electrical system at a high school. Dr. Roger's wife, Brenda, goes over to the mental health center every Friday to help and next year she will start a teaching program at the center. We're appalled by the lack of decent clothing for the patients. The problem is that when they get new clothing, they hand it out the window to a relative so that they'll have something to wear when they get out. There's a great need for sheets and all kinds of medical supplies. Right

126

now we have two of our work party in Georgetown on St. Vincent making an evaluation of what is needed as a result of the closing of the island's sugar operation. I could go on."

"I get the picture." I said.

June described their dilemma. "Ron and I have gone about as far as we can with the energy that we have. Frankly, we are worried. Will the Bequia Mission and all the things we are trying to do end when we no longer have the energy? We've got about five years, God willing, but that's it."

"We have started to look for people to take over. We found two young people in their thirties, who were part of a work party, and they fell in love with Bequia. Maybe they represent the future of the Mission."

"We'll probably have to change our philosophy," June said. "We've been an unpaid volunteer organization. That might not work after we're gone."

I tended to agree with them but I didn't say anything. It seemed a pity to me that they couldn't be cloned and thereby guarantee the survival of the Mission. To hire a paid staff will require a substantial increase in the Mission's budget and that will probably require fund raising help, and now all of a sudden it will be a very different kind of organization. Ron and June supply zeal and love that may be irreplaceable.

Judy appeared on the scene to talk with her parents. A fine-looking girl, with lots of energy like her parents, I thought. Judy had married a Bequian, Mac Simmons. When they first started their restaurant, Judy named it Gracious Goodness. That was a little much for Mac and so they renamed it Mac's Pizza. She went along with the change quite

127

willingly. When you live on the island, you learn how important it is for the male to be out front. They have two children, a very successful business in which they are both involved, and what appears to be a pleasant and happy life. What happens when the children are of school age? That's hard to say. Others on the island have sent their children to boarding schools in Barbados and abroad.

After leaving the restaurant, Ron, June and I walked back toward the harbor and stopped for a moment at the Workshop for the Handicapped. Inside were six men and women making wooden souvenirs for the tourist trade. I bought a couple of whales to take home.

One of the handicapped, Dafton, used to dive for lobster and conch. One day he dove very deeply and came back to the surface too quickly and got the bends. Others have been crippled and at least one died, Seaton Gregg of Paget Farm. Ron's and June's response was to start a school for divers, which they named the Seaton Gregg Memorial School for Divers. With the help of Diver Bob, a professional diver who takes tourists on diving expeditions, instruction was given in the skill of diving and maintaining equipment to anyone who was interested. Last year 21 young people attended the school and received certificates as qualified divers. Glenroy Adams was sent to the United States to receive training and certification as a diving instructor. He is now back on Bequia and in charge of the Divers' School.

THE WALLACHS

Violet Wallach and I were sitting on the terrace of the Frangipani, looking out to sea, waiting for Jimmy Carville, alias Santa Claus, to come into view in his gift-laden rubber raft. Santa was making his first trip to Bequia, and from where I sat I could see a crowd of several hundred youngsters already assembled on the jetty. Jimmy had started his trip from La Pomp, half way around the other side of the island, earlier in the morning. I had been with him in the early morning taking photographs. Bulu, a deaf black boy, was with Jimmy in the raft. Jimmy later explained that in the Dutch tradition Santa was usually accompanied by a black boy dressed in gold and white.

I had been talking with Violet about the work that Jimmy was doing to help deaf children.

"It all started with Bulu," Violet said. "He did a terrific job with that boy. Bulu can read lips and people don't think he is crazy anymore.''

"I understand that Jimmy went around door-to-door to find out if there were any more deaf children like Bulu,'' I said.

"He found eight, maybe nine or ten,'' she said. "He has all of them over his house every morning learning to lip read.''

I long ago realized that Violet made it a point to keep on top of everything taking place on the island. She wasn't a gossip. Sometimes she was accused of being that, and that was wrong. She was genuinely more interested in people than most others. In other words, she really cared.

She and her husband, Rolf, helped in many ways. They helped stock the library at Paget Farms School, underwrote many children at school, and gave liberally to almost every cause. They were responsible for at least twenty scholarships at the high school.

"When we had guests at our house, we asked them not to tip our maid, whom we took good care of,'' Violet explained. "We suggested an alternative. If they paid for a child's tuition for one semester at the high school, which was $25, we would pay for the remaining two semesters. It worked fine.''

Violet liked to wear simple dresses, with small flower prints, that the Bequia women made. She liked to play down the way she looked. just as she liked to play down what she did for people. You wouldn't think that a woman so slight and in her seventies could get around the way Violet did.

"I wonder what's taking them so long,'' Violet said, squinting as she searched the harbor for Jimmy's rubber raft.

130

"They'll get wet if they go too fast," I said.

Earlier in the morning Violet and Rolf had taken many cartons of Christmas gifts to the school auditorium for Santa to hand out. They were in addition to those that Jimmy and Bulu would carry. Violet and Rolf had brought the cartons down with them from Connecticut. Rolf was in the business of importing handicrafts from Europe, so he had easy access to toys of all kinds.

"I want to see the look on the children's faces when they meet Santa for the first time," she said. "We never had our own. And for that I am very sorry."

I thought I saw her eyes glisten.

"It's sad these kids have so little," she said.

"They get a big bang out of what they have," I said. "Rolling a hoop down a hill, guiding it with a stick, seems to give them great pleasure."

Violet loved to spend time with children. She always carried something with her that she could give them. Candy, gum, pencils, erasers, coins in small denominations. If a child came to her and begged, she would scold him gently. She would say "Bequia children do not beg. It is wrong. What would your mother or father say if they knew? Now if you would like to run an errand for me, I will pay you something." Her approach usually worked.

In addition to the hundreds of toys they brought down, Violet solicited money from the local merchants to buy candies and cookies. She wasn't bashful about asking for money and her persistence usually wore down any resistance. She had become very successful at this since her first fund raising in behalf of the deaf children. Jimmy had worked with the children in his home for about six months and felt the need for assistance. He persuaded a young girl named Avala, who had graduated with honors from schools on Bequia and St. Vincent, to help out. Jimmy realized he couldn't ask her to work on a volunteer basis, so he enlisted Violet's help. As a result of her efforts, enough money was raised to pay Avala a modest salary for a year. After that Father Ron Armstrong became involved and started the School for the Deaf. He sent Avala to Canada to study sign language and when she returned she headed up the school.

Violet's attention was caught by the many large yachts in the harbor for the holidays.

"There've been many changes since I first came to the island," she said.

"When was that?"

"About thirty years ago. There were few boats then and the jetty didn't exist. Most of them were native boats. They were small and had no problem coming ashore. The beach stretched all the way from the harbor to the Sunny Caribee and people used the beach as a road. There was only one taxi and William Gooding ran it. Ladies never wore shorts or slacks into the harbor out of respect for local customs."

"Still the island is as beautiful as it ever was," I said.

"And the people are just as friendly," she added. "I think that what I like best is their friendliness. I remember my first trip. I was caught in the harbor in a storm and I didn't know where to go for shelter. A woman came over to me and took me by the hand. 'Ya don wanna get wet, Mistress,' she said and led me to the protection of the Peoples Store, which, by the way, was the only store on the island then. I love the people here. They'll do anything for you, if you treat them with respect.''

"What brought you here?'' I asked.

"Rolf and I were visiting Grenada,'' she said. "I heard that the island had no electricity and no telephones. I was told that the beaches were nice and the people were friendly, so we came over. We stayed at the Sunny Caribee. You wouldn't believe the rates. Ten dollars a day and that included coffee or tea brought to your room in the morning, breakfast, lunch, afternoon tea, and dinner. Tom and Glady ran the Sunny Caribee. Then they bought Moonhole and they invited us to come and stay with them. We fell in love with the place and Rolf gave Tom a down payment of a thousand dollars to build us a home. We were the first on Moonhole after the Johnstons. Years later we sold our house to Walter Weir, the advertising executive.''

"We loved Moonhole. It's a very unusual place,'' she added. "We were visited once by the Queen of England. She came in her yacht and they were anchored on the lee side of Moonhole. Her Lady in Waiting and the Captain came ashore. They asked if the Queen could swim here and we said of course she could. We offered them our home to use for changing. The sea roughened up and they came back and apologized and said the Queen was very poor on the sea. She doesn't go down steps to get in a boat like everybody else. They lower her in a chair. She never came ashore but dispatched a very lovely letter, which I've still got.''

"After Moonhole, we stayed at the Anthony Eden house,'' she continued. "For most people the name probably suggests something very big and lavish. But it isn't. It's the simplest of homes. It is typically West Indian.''

Violet and Rolf have gotten in the habit of coming to Bequia every year, arriving usually in November and returning to their home in Connecticut in April. During this period Rolf makes two trips to Europe to purchase handicrafts which he sells to gift stores, particularly at Christmas. They stay now at the Sunny Caribee, but when Rolf is away on business, Violet shifts to Julie's Guest House, which is smaller, very comfortable, and, most important, in the middle of everything.

Rolf was born in Munich, where his family owned Wallachs, a very large and elegant emporium, which specialized in handicrafts from the countries of Europe and looked more like a museum than a store. Rolf went into the family business in 1929, when he was twenty, and quickly realized that he was not needed. He came to the States to get experience and expected to stay only a few years.

"My father thought it was a nutty idea,'' Rolf has said. "But he didn't oppose it.''

Rolf worked in a factory and he was an errand boy for a hat firm on 28th Street in Manhattan. He had planned to return to Munich in 1931 "when the Hitler thing started and I decided to stay in the States until that blew over. By 1935 I realized it was not going to blow over and I became a naturalized citizen.''

Rolf married Violet earlier, in 1932, and they moved from the East Side in New York to Jackson Heights. He got a job with a tool factory and stayed in that job through the war. He started his import business just after the war, moved to Wingdale, New York, and then to Sherman, Connecticut.

"When I became a naturalized citizen in 1935 I realized the dream of returning to my father's business was over," Rolf said. "The Nazis took it over and gave it to a man named Witte, who was an official in Munich."

But that story had a happy ending. When the American Occupation Forces held restitution hearings concerning properties that had been confiscated by the Nazis, Rolf's father's lawyer was able to produce a letter from Witte written before the war stating that if he didn't turn over the business to him, he would find himself in a concentration camp within 24 hours. The business was promptly returned to the Wallach family, where it remained until 1986, when it was sold.

I asked Violet where and how she met Rolf.

"It was fate, an accident of fate," she said. "I went to Germany with my mother. There was a girl named Hilda who was leader of the hiking group. We spent much time together and became pals. Some years later I visited Hilda in Long Island City and there I met Rolf. Hilda's mother and Rolf's mother were cousins. That was in 1932. I was 24. I married Rolf the same year."

I was reminded of a book that Violet had showed me back in the States. It was an album of photographs of the Wallach and related families. It was a big book published by Knopf. The captions identified the people in the photographs who had survived the holocaust and those who had not. In some photographs there were no survivors. Mention of 1932 triggered that recollection, which lasted only a moment, crowded out by the rising level of noise from the anxious, waiting Bequians.

The rubber raft carrying Jimmy Carville and Bulu turned

the point and now came into view. Violet and I hurried to the jetty and got there as they came ashore. They were greeted with whistles, shouts, and thunderous applause. The procession to the school auditorium started up and Violet and I joined the mass of happy, noisy children and their equally happy and noisy parents, led by a steel band on top of Big Wheels, a truck used normally for hauling.

Violet stood closeby as Santa and Bulu handed out the presents to the children in the school auditorium. Occasionally a parent slipped into the waiting line. It wasn't unexpected, and Jimmy had a suitable present. Tears came into Violet's eyes, as she watched the happy children.

BLESSING OF THE WHALEBOATS

The whaling season officially starts with the blessing of
the whaleboats late in January when the hump backs pass
between Bequia and Mustique, about eight miles away, on
their way farther south to breed. A large crowd had already
collected around the two whaleboats, Dart and Why Ask?,
on the beach at Friendship. I noticed many familiar faces:
Tom Johnston, Jimmy Carville, Violet Wallach, Father Ron
Armstrong, June Armstrong, Nobleman. The twelve whalers
and the two spotters were there, and in the center of the
crowd, Athneal Ollivierre. From where I stood — I looked
down on them from a slightly higher level — Athneal looked
small and frail, hardly the intrepid warrior who would jump
on top of a whale to drive a lance deeper into its body. He
moved among the members of his crews and the guests. He
was shy and retiring, except when the subject was whaling.

It was another beautiful day, with hardly a cloud in the

137

sky, and the trade winds blew steadily from the east, pushing the sea into waves that broke close to shore. Behind us were seine nets drying in the sun and farther along the beach many small fishing boats with their sails neatly furled and resting on the decks. Birds raced along the beach picking up food, washed up by the waves. There were kids in the water, playing. Their sleek brown bodies glistened in the sun.

The ceremony was about to start and the crowd quieted.

Father Armstrong wore his white robe with gold sash. He looked a lot younger than his sixty years. He held a bible in one hand and a bottle of holy water in the other. He stood at the bow of Why Ask? and proceeded to bless the holy water, "...and wheresoever it shall be sprinkled, there let the presence of the Holy Ghost be vouchsafed to all of us who shall ask for mercy. Amen."

A group of children from the Anglican Church at Paget began to sing. The selection was a favorite of the whalers, "For Those in Peril on the Sea." Their voices were clear and true and their brown faces sparkled.

Father Armstrong then read from Genesis, establishing God's authority to have dominion over the creatures of the sea. "Be fruitful and multiply and fill the earth and subdue it, and have dominion over the fish of the sea and over the birds of the air and over everything that move upon the earth."

The people were so quiet and still that those fifty feet away could hear the Father and even the sea seemed quieter and gentler than usual.

"Then they cried to the Lord in their trouble," Father said, reading from the 107th Psalm, "and he delivered them from their distress; he made the storm be still and the waves of the sea were hushed ..."

Jesus takes authority over the storm as Father reads from Matthew 9, "Why are you afraid, O men of little faith? Then he rose and rebuked the winds and the sea and there was a great calm."

The time for the blessing was now at hand. All strained to watch Father.

"Be favorable, O Lord, unto our prayers, and with thy right hand bless this boat and all who shall voyage therein; stretch forth unto them thy holy arm to be their protection as thou didst stretch it forth unto blessed Peter when he walked upon the sea, and do thou send thy holy Angel from heaven to keep and deliver this vessel from every peril, together with those who voyage therein: and graciously behold thy servants, that all perils being done away, they may by a favorable course come to a fair haven; and their business ended, return rejoicing to their own homes. Who livest and reignest, God, world without end. Amen."

"Amen," the people echoed.

Father sprinkled holy water first at the bow and then at the stern. He repeated the ceremony for the second whaleboat. He blessed Athneal and the other whalers. In his closing prayer, he asked for their safety and for good hunting. At this point Athneal brought forth a bottle of rum, poured a tot, and spilled it on the bow of Why Ask? and then repeated the ceremony for Dart.

The ceremony and the quiet were now over. People began milling about and lining up to wish Athneal good luck. Wives of the whalers brought food and drink down to the beach and set up tables around the whaleboats. The food included chicken parts, salads, curried rice, planten and coconut. Most people on the island drink rum, so that was the only hard liquor served. They wandered around the boats and ate from paper plates and talked. Several bottles of strong rum were brought out and the conversations got livelier as the rum was consumed.

I noticed Tom Johnston talking with Athneal and I joined them.

"I hear there's going to be a whaling museum," I said.

"Looks that way," Athneal replied.

His laconic reply reminded me of a New England fisherman. He looked different from the man I observed standing at a higher level. Weatherbeaten, sinewy. More like a whaler.

"Who is going to build it?"

"I will," said Tom, "if they let me have my way."

"Who is they?"

"The committee."

"They have one of those?"

"Well, it's Pat Mitchell's project and she formed a committee.

Violet got into the conversation.

"Where will it be?"

"Across the street from my house," Athneal replied.

"Maybe," Tom said.

"I'm donating a lot of my equipment," Athneal replied. "I guess I'll have something to say."

"I'll help with the fund raising," Violet said.

"The Engleheart sisters said they would finance it," Tom said.

140

"Oh," Violet responded with obvious disappointment.

"It's a great idea," I said. "Great for tourism."

"The idea is for the whalers to benefit," Tom said. "Athneal and his group are the last of the whalers. There's nobody to step into their shoes when they get too old. The museum will give them money to live on."

"How much longer do you think they will go on whaling?" I asked.

"Not too much longer," Tom said. "Athneal is getting on."

Jimmy entered the conversation.

"What's your timetable?" he asked.

"You can't have a timetable on Bequia," Violet admonished Jimmy.

Jimmy laughed.

"You're right, of course."

"Where's Sandy?" I asked.

"He's packing. We're going back for a couple of months. We've got a group of students coming down in June."

"Big group?"

"Average. We expect fourteen."

I turned around and saw Nobleman and motioned him over. "Have you got your taxi here?"

"Top of the hill."

"I'll want a ride back."

"I'll watch for you," Nobleman said and left.

"This is the first blessing I've attended," I said.

"The whalers really believe in them," Jimmy said. "After the blessing last year, Athneal said he had never seen so many whales.''

"I don't remember that they caught any," I said.

"You're right and it worried Athneal. I understand that he told Father Armstrong that there was crosstalk, meaning that some people were praying that he wouldn't catch any."

Father Armstrong joined the group.

"He was plenty worried. He asked me to pray for him and his crew. I said I would."

"What happened?" I asked.

"They caught one two days later," Jimmy said.

"That's quite a testimonial," I said.

Father smiled.

"I've got to be going," I said, "Can I give anyone a ride?"

There were no takers. On the way up to the road, I turned around and looked down on the crowd. I thought it was kind of nice that so many people from different backgrounds could get together like this and share in the seriousness and the fun of a blessing ceremony. I couldn't think of anything back home that would have the same meaning and effect.

Bequia had left its mark on each of them, I thought. "You, too, Nobleman," I said as I got into his cab.

"Huh?"

"It's a great island."

"Ah, yes."

SUMMING UP

There are many more people on Bequia I would like to introduce to you. Their stories are like the others in a least one respect: this island, this unspoiled, and beautiful island has given their lives a meaning that did not exist before. To some it is Shangri-la. Somewhat lower on the scale of meaning, it offers the opportunity to be yourself and to enjoy life on a belly-to-belly basis with nature. For others it is an escape from the frustrations, inequities, and tedium of the modern world.

When I was digging for artifacts on the beach at Park Estate, I thought of Bill and Elan Smith. Bill has collected many pieces of Arawak pottery from this beach and, like working with a jig saw puzzle, has succeeded in putting them together to form plates and saucers and jugs of all kinds. Bill plans to use the artifacts as decorations in the new home that he is building at Friendship Bay.

Bill came to the island many years ago. His first experience was during the war when his naval vessel searched the waters for German U-Boats. He returned after the war to the Grenadines and, like others, made a mental note that he would one day come back. Some years later, after an unsuccessful marriage to one of the Buckley's, he met Elan, a southern belle, married her and they emigrated to Bequia.

Bill is a part-time entrepreneur. He dabbles in real estate with moderate success. He has come a cropper on occasion when dealing with local mores. I remember one occasion when a contestant threatened to have a curse placed on him. Such a thing is a serious matter on Bequia. Bill, fortunately, was planning to return to the States for a short visit, and simply accelerated his plans.

Bill has done some research on the Arawak civilization that once dominated South America and the islands. Legend has it that the Arawaks existed as long ago as 5000 BC. They were peaceful, intelligent, and primarily agrarian. An offshoot was a tribe called the Charibs, which means rebellious. They conquered the Arawaks, killed the males, and intermarried with the females. According to Bill, the Charibs, or Caribs, as they are now called, occupied Martinique, Dominica, St. Lucia, and St. Vincent. Bill believes there are many potential digs on Bequia, which he hopes to find and develop.

The loveliest inn on the island is Spring Hotel, located on Spring Plantation, about two miles from the harbor. It was once a plantation house, which a group of five Iowans acquired in the mid 1960s along with about 85 acres. They made an inn out of it with ten rooms for guests. About eight years ago Dick Rudolf, a stamp collector from Minneapolis, bought it and turned it over to his daughter, Candy, and her husband, Rosey (short for Roosevelt), to manage.

Rosey is a Leslie, of whom there are many living on Mt. Pleasant. Candy has become very involved with the Leslies. If there are no guests at Spring, Sunday is a day to be spent with Rosey, their two children, and the Leslie family on Mt. Pleasant.

Candy, who speaks fluent Chinese, runs the hotel in a lay-back manner. It appears that success does not mean a full house throughout the tourist season. Fewer guests, who can be accommodated without a lot of hubbub, appear to be more in keeping with the Leslie's relaxed style of hotel management. It is a family operation. Rosey is in charge of the kitchen. Candy runs the hotel. Rosey's father manages the plantation, which grows coconuts, bananas, and many vegetables and fruits. Candy's father, back in Minneapolis, drums up business.

For some unexplainable reason, Canadians in particular appear to be attracted to the island. In addition to Father Armstrong and his wife, June, and Dr. Eric Rodgers, and his wife, Brenda, there are many other Canadians, Such as Helen, who married Clyde Gooding, a marine mechanic who plays a banjo in his free time with a local band, and Edie, wife to Stedman Wallace, who owns the dry goods store in the harbor. The island has attracted many nationalities, German, Scandinavian, English, Belgian, South American, and American. Bruno Fink, a German, is proprietor of the Bequia Beach Club at Friendship Bay and Eduardo Guadagnino, owner of Friendship Bay Hotel, is from

Argentina, via California, where his wife, Joanne, was born. The Mustadts at Industry Estate are from Norway. Garnis, an ex-model from Seattle, of Scandinavian ancestry, conducts aerobic classes at Friendship Hotel and occasionally gives haircuts on the beach attired in her sarong, which makes a great picture. Sam McDowell, an artist from California, has a home near Paget Farms and spends a few months of the year painting local scenes. Prints of his paintings can usually be found in the bookstore, which is run by Ian and Cyralene Gale, who came to Bequia from Trinidad via Barbados. Dick Burke's main contribution to the island is the Parish Workshop, which he started, financed, and equipped. Jim, a Bequian, runs the Workshop and makes a number of products needed on the island, such as bathtubs, small boats, cabinets, most anything made of wood and plastics. The profits of the workshop go to Jim and the parish. The Burkes live at Moonhole. Their daughter, Molly, once ran the Whalebone Bar, which was featured in Look Magazine in 1960.

Adapting to the culture of the island is both easy and difficult. The island is slow to change, which is its charm for many. The flip side is that it takes a long time for new ideas to be accepted. For example, not everyone accepts the fact that the United States put a man on the moon. A defense for old ways of doing things is, ''But das de way we duz it.''

There are no golf courses or casinos, so it is not everyone's island. There are only four inns and they are small. The only entertainment are the jump-ups that are held several nights a week at the inns in the tourist season. For the most part you make your own entertainment and you can usually

146

count on good weather and star-lit nights. There are many beaches and the fishing is good and conditions are perfect for sailing.

The people are proud of their brightly colored but modest homes. There is no poverty on the island but some live humbly. The children are dressed in uniforms for school and on Sundays the whole family puts on its best for church. You have nothing to fear on the island. You can be anywhere at any hour of the day or night and feel safe. You can walk the two miles from Spring to the harbor at five in the morning to catch the Friendship Rose and the people you meet in the dark are your friends.

To make the adjustment to the island, you must be willing to accept the fact that jumbies do exist, at least in the Bequian's mind. If he has not seen a jumbie, he at least knows someone who has. There's a small stone bridge half way between Spring and the harbor called Jumbie Bridge. There's a jumbie named Friday who lives under the bridge. His name is Friday because when he lived in the early 1800s it was his job to meet out punishment to the slaves on Friday. The women who work at Spring will not walk across the bridge at night. The reason why all windows are shuttered tight at night is to keep the jumbies and the night air out.

There are many stories about obeah, a form of medicine practiced by what we would call witch doctors. Stories are frequently told in the form of songs, as for example:

Papa Lou-Lou fool me an' turn me pappy-show,
Ah feeling so ashame ah doan want nobody know.
'E say dey put a jumbie lizard in me belly,

147

An' e' say 'e want a cattle calf fo' tek un outa me.
Never never me again believe in obeah man,
No no no no no no believe in obeah man.
We went up to 'petani - the story sound so true
An' carrying me cattle-calf fo' Papa Lou-Lou
'E tek me in a dark room dis trickey obeah man,
An 'e start to wuk 'e obeah wid a candle in 'e han'.
'E pull a little basket from underneath 'e bed
An' telling me doan frighten, an' turn away me head.
'E open up de basket - ah nearly faint away,
When Papa Lou-Lou pull out a living Cocoa-bay.
Shame! Papa Lou-Lou, you' ha' no sympathy,
To rob me of me cattle-calf, a poor woman like me.

A Cocoa-bay, incidentally, is a very large lizard. An obeah man is still important on the island. Many prefer to see him first before the clinic's medical doctor.

The moon is very important. Bequians plant by the phase of the moon and they fish by the moon and if you cut bamboo in the wrong phase, it will disintegrate. They are correct more often than wrong.

For those who have been able to adjust to the island's culture, living on Bequia is a unique experience. The Carib name for St. Vincent is Haroun, which means the island of the blessed. It would be more fitting if applied to Bequia.

There are some pitfalls living in paradise. It can become monotonous. When perfect weather continues on and on endlessly it sometimes prompts the response, "Another rotten day in paradise," which is said in humor, rather than derogation. The obvious answer to the threat of boredom is to have sufficient interests to keep you busy. Don't count on golf, there isn't any. Tennis is okay. Deep sea diving, fishing, sailing, swimming, wind-surfing, gardening, partying, gossiping, running, walking, napping, observing, these are all okay.

Curiosity is probably the best defense. It is all a marvelous wonder. The sea pounds relentless and noisily against the shore. The air is so fresh, fragrant, and smooth as silk. The flowers seem to bloom endlessly. The stars at night come closer daring you to reach to touch. The weather is perfect for at least ten of the twelve months. Everything comes together in a nice fit and if you are lucky you belong.

Like a sea anemone, the magic of Bequia has many tendrils and it is so pleasant when you are caught.